THE ULTIMATE GUIDE TO

FRYING

THE ULTIMATE GUIDE TO

How to Fry Just About Anything

RICK BROWNE

Skyhorse Publishing

Skyhorse Publishing books may be purchased in bulk at special discounts for sales promotion, corporate gifts, fund-raising, or educational purposes. Special editions can also be created to specifications. For details, contact the Special Sales Department, Skyhorse Publishing, 555 Eighth Avenue, Suite 903, New York, NY 10018 or info@skyhorsepublishing.com.

www.skyhorsepublishing.com

10 9 8 7 6 5 4 3 2 1

Library of Congress Cataloging-in-Publication Data

Browne, Rick, 1946-
  The ultimate guide to frying : how to fry just about anything / Rick Browne.
      p. cm.
  Includes index.
  ISBN 978-1-61608-066-2 (pbk. : alk. paper)
  1. Frying. I. Title.
  TX689.B765 2010
  641.7'7–dc22
                              2010017485
Printed in China

I would like to dedicate this book to four
special people:

My mom, Dorothy, for instilling in me
the love of good home-cooked food and the
fun of cooking it.

My dad, Arnold, for instilling in me the
love of travel, of going to new places, and
meeting wonderful, new people around every
bend in the road.

My brother Grant, for taking me on
hikes and nature walks, thus instilling in
me the love of outdoors, of the wonders of
nature, and the mystery of all the creatures
that inhabit it.

And my lovely wife, Kathy, for believing
in me, for helping me fulfill a lifelong desire
to travel the backroads of America, and
who shares my love of cooking, making new
friends, and enjoying life to the fullest.

Contents

Introduction

FREQUENT FRYERS BEWARE!

Deep fat frying has been with us as almost as long as the discovery that fire would make raw meat taste a whole lot better. In fact, cooking food in various oil or fats is still the only way they cook in some countries, societies, and single-guy apartments.

And deep-frying, in large pots, has been practiced in many parts of the country for years. While frying a whole turkey is fairly new to many of us, Southern folks and Texans have been doin' it for decades. "Deep-fried" surely began in an Alabama kitchen somewhere.

Our aim here is to demystify the process and reveal the culinary delights of this style of cooking. But recently a pall has been spread over the world of deep-frying, spawned by a few vocal, overzealous, and overprotective folks who think those of us who have—or wish to purchase—deep-frying equipment don't have the brains God gave a newt.

Sure there are safety issues so you won't burn down your garage, deck, or house. But all of those, and I do mean ALL, can be addressed and dismissed with a liberal application of what we Americans are best known for (in most cases anyway): COMMON SENSE.

Add some frying recipes and some helpful hints and techniques that we offer up here, and there should be NO problem deep-frying that turkey, roast, game hen, prawn, or donut. Attempts without proper preparation using a propane burner to boil several gallons of oil can be hazardous. But following the manufacturer's suggestions, having the good sense to pick up and read this book, and using your brain for something other than holding your ears apart will ensure a safe, fun, and delicious experience as a frequent fryer!

Deep Fat Frying Basics

DEEP-FRYING TIPS

✪ Maintain a frying temperature of 375°F (190°C). That way the battered, breaded surfaces will quickly form a protective shield, keeping the oil from penetrating the food as it cools and keeping it grease-free.

✳ DO NOT SALT FOOD before deep-frying. Salt draws moisture to the surface, which can splatter when the food is added to the hot oil. Salt also lowers the smoke point and breaks the oil down more quickly. Only add salt just before eating, if at all.

✪ Dip the food into lightly-beaten egg and then roll it in seasoned bread crumbs. Allow the uncooked breaded food to rest on a rack at room temperature for 15–20 minutes before frying so that the food can partially dry and the crumbs adhere to the food.

✪ Have the eggs at room temperature and avoid beating them too much. Air bubbles in over-whisked eggs form pockets on the food when it's dipped into the egg. These pockets won't take breading.

✳ If the oil is too hot, the coating will burn from the intense heat of the oil before the food inside the batter/coating has had time to cook properly. Burned outside, and semi-raw inside: Not a good thing!

✪ Don't jam the fryer with food; things need space to cook properly, and too much food will lower the oil's temperature.

✳ Small bread crumbs are much better than large breads crumbs.

✪ For each portion of food, use at least six volumes of oil.

✳ Preheat the oil to about 7 to 8°C (15°F) higher than its optimal deep-frying temperature. This is to allow for the immediate cooling of the oil when food is added. Preheating it higher than this may damage the oil's molecular structure.

RECOMMENDED FRYING & DEEP-FRYING OILS

DEEP FRY:

Peanut Oil is good if you want to fry every day with the same oil, but it should be used only for a few hours per day.

Sunflower Oil can be used if you fry the whole day continuously with the same oil. But after this one day of extensive use, it might have to be replaced.

SHALLOW FRY:

Coconut Fat is good for frying if it is not hydrogenated (hardened). Hydrogenated fats and oils are extremely dangerous for your health and should be omitted from a healthy diet because they contain harmful trans-fatty acids.

Clarified Butter is very good for frying, but it is more expensive than most oils.

Olive Oil contains many monounsaturated fatty acids and is good for pan frying, but not for the rigors of extensive deep fat frying.

Canola Oil made from rapeseed is used extensively in food service.

HOW LONG WILL FRYING OIL LAST?

The longer you use oil, the more it starts to oxidize and deteriorate. It's important, between frying sessions, to filter it, store it in a cool location, and protect it from light. All of these help prolong its life.

The hotter oil gets, the faster it begins to decompose and fail. Don't cook at 375°F if your recipe suggests 325°F.

If food particles are not filtered out frequently, they tend to burn and can not only cause the oil to fail more quickly, but can also form toxic chemicals in the oil. Filter after each use when you pour the oil back into its storage container.

Eating too many fried preparations and using oxidized or spoiled oils can cause minor to severe health problems.

When oil becomes deteriorated, it appears dark and thick (viscous). It may have an off odor, and smoke appears before it reaches 375°F. If the oil smells funky and old, better to toss it away and replace it with fresh oil.

Filter deep fat fryer oil every time you use it!

SMOKE POINTS OF OILS

Knowing the smoke point of the oil you intend to cook with is important because each time you deep fry, you lower its smoke point irreversibly. The smoke point is the temperature at which the oil begins to break down and to smoke. When the oil breaks down, it is unusable for cooking.

If your oil's smoke point is just above 375°F (190°C), which is the normal deep-frying temperature, chances are its smoke point will drop below 375°F (190°C) after its first use, rendering it useless for further deep-frying.

If you want to save money by reusing an oil as many times as possible, select one with a high smoke point.

A number of factors will decrease the smoke point of any oil:

- « combination of vegetable oils in products
- « foreign properties in oil (crumbs from batter)
- « temperature to which oil is heated
- « presence of salt
- « number of times oil is used
- « length of time oil is heated
- « exposure to oxygen and light during storage
- « temperature at which oil is stored

OIL SMOKE POINTS

Safflower	265°C	509°F
Sunflower	246°C	475°F
Soybean	241°C	465°F
Canola	238°C	460°F
Corn	236°C	457°F
Peanut	231°C	448°F
Sesame	215°C	419°F
Olive	190°C	374°F

Knowing the smoke point will also warn you about the flash and fire points.

An oil reaches its **flash point** (about 600°F [320°C] for most oils) when tiny wisps of fire begin to leap from its surface. You do not want to get to this point.

If the oil is heated to its **fire point** (slightly under 700°F [400°C] for most oils), its surface will be ablaze, and you have a big problem at hand.

NEVER use water to put out an oil fire: the water will splatter the burning oil and spread it more quickly. Instead, smother the flames with a tight-fitting lid or sheet of aluminum foil. If the fire has spread outside the pan, suffocate it with baking soda or a fire extinguisher formulated for oil fires.

PROLONGING OIL'S USEFUL LIFE

The longer an oil is heated, the more quickly it will decompose, so avoid preheating the oil any longer than necessary. If you're frying more than one batch of anything, quickly add each new batch, unless you need more time to bring the temperature back up. Turn off the heat as soon as you've finished cooking.

Use a quality deep fat frying thermometer.

Shake off loose break crumbs from breaded food before cooking. Crumbs and other particles scorch quickly and will speed up the demise of your oil. Use a small strainer, a strainer lined with a paper towel, or a slotted spoon to remove as many crumbs as you can.

Do not mix used oil with fresh oil.

When the oil has cooled enough that it is safe to handle, strain it through paper towels, coffee filters, or cheesecloth (or two of these in succession) into its original empty container or a clear glass jar.

Store the oil, tightly sealed, in a cool, dark place or in the refrigerator. The oil may cloud in the refrigerator, but it will become clear again at room temperature.

TIME TO CHANGE THE OIL?

Oil darkens with use because the oil itself, and tiny food particles in it, burn when put to a high heat.

The more you use an oil, the more slowly it will pour. Its viscosity changes because of changes to the oil's molecular structure. When it pours like ketchup, throw it out!

Loose food particles collect as sediment at the bottom of the container you're storing oil in, or float in the oil.

When smoke appears on the surface of the oil before the temperature reaches 375°F (190°C), your oil is no good.

If the oil has a rancid smell or if it smells like the foods you've cooked in it, throw it away. There's nothing worse than cooking a turkey in fish-smelling oil, or vice versa.

TIME & TEMPERATURE GUIDELINES

FOR DEEP FAT FRYING

VEGETABLES:

ITEM	TEMP.	FRYING TIME
French Fries, Raw	360°F	5–6 minutes
French Fries, Frozen	360°F	4–5 minutes
French Fries, Frozen, Blanched	360°F	3–4 minutes
Onion Rings, Breaded, Fresh	360°F	3–4 minutes
Onion Rings, Breaded, Frozen	360°F	4–5 minutes
Assorted Vegetables, Breaded	360°F	5–6 minutes
Vegetable Fritters	360°F	6–8 minutes

SEAFOOD:

ITEM	TEMP.	FRYING TIME
Fish Filet, Breaded, Fresh	360°F	3–4 minutes
Fish Filet, Breaded, Frozen	360°F	4–5 minutes
Shrimp, Breaded, Fresh	360°F	3–4 minutes
Shrimp, Breaded, Frozen	360°F	4–5 minutes
Oysters, Breaded	360°F	3–4 minutes
Clams, Breaded, Strips	360°F	1.5 minutes
Scallops, Breaded, Frozen	360°F	4 minutes

BREADED MEATS:

ITEM	TEMP.	FRYING TIME
Cutlet, Breaded, Frozen	360°F	5–6 minutes
Chicken, Breaded, Large	360°F	10–14 minutes
Chicken, Breaded, Small	360°F	8–12 minutes

SWEET ITEMS:

ITEM	TEMP.	FRYING TIME
Yeast-Raised Donuts	375°F	3 minutes
Cake Donuts	375°F	2–2.5 minutes
Fruit-Filled Fritters	360°F	5–7 minutes

DEEP FAT FRYING WITHOUT A THERMOMETER

Temperature and time at which a 1-inch cube of white bread will turn golden brown:

345°–355° ..... 65 seconds
355°–365° ..... 60 seconds
365°–375° ..... 50 seconds
375°–385° ..... 40 seconds
385°–395° ..... 20 seconds
395°–400° ..... 10 seconds

Deep-frying a Whole Turkey

A DUMB BIRD IS HE

The domesticated turkey is perhaps the dumbest animal on the planet, next to perhaps gooney birds, paper clips, and lawn mold. But it's not their fault. It's because they've been bred and re-bred, generation after generation, in captivity. Darwin's Laws of Natural Selection and Variation don't work when some bozo wearing horn-rimmed glasses and thongs feeds you, raises you, protects you, houses you, nurtures you, and then kills you. To be kind, one can say that they lack "street savvy," or in this case even "turkey-pen savvy."

But over and above that they're fat, weak, and probably couldn't fend for themselves if they were allowed to fend. They're clumsy, they're slower than a three-legged turtle, and, in a bid to prevent escapes from that turkey pen, each and every last one of 'em has been bred to not be able to fly. Sad to say they ain't much but good eatin'.

Two hundred seventy six million turkeys were raised in the United States in 2001.

Continuing our dissing of the birds: Turkeys are insecure, panic easily, and get "all het up" at the slightest change in their environment. Watch what happens in a flock of turkeys if you make a loud noise—instant bedlam, almost like a 75% (no, 90%) discount sale in lady's shoes at Nordstrom Rack.

If there were turkey psychologists they'd make a fortune. When frightened, gazillions of frantic and frenetic birds run around in circles and flee

smack dab into the nearest corner, wooden fence, or barn. And then dozens more birds behind *them* charge full speed into the same corner, fence or barn and everyone ends up in a big pile of broken turkeys, the maimed and crippled ones on top smothering those even unluckier birds at the bottom.

Turkeys were first domesticated on our shores by Southwest Indians 2,000 years ago.

And guess what else? Turkeys have heart attacks. The United States Air Force was doing test runs and breaking the sound barrier near a turkey farm, where hundreds of turkeys dropped dead with heart attacks.

Urban legend aside, there are somewhat reliable—if you believe the old "I-know-people-who-know-people-who-saw-them"—kinda stories, of young birds opening their thirsty mouths to raindrops pouring from the sky, but forgetting to close them and drowning in the one last quench of thirst. But we don't believe those stories. . . . naaaah!

Wild turkeys can fly for short distances up to 55 miles per hour.

By the way, the bird's name is another mistake. A long time ago some folks thought the funny looking birds came from—you guessed it—Turkey, when really they'd been here for years. But some dolt somehow got the idea that turkeys were guinea fowl that came from Islamic "Turkish" lands, and passed that on to someone else.

A few experts think the first Thanksgiving dinner was served·by the Pilgrims sometime between September 21 and November 9, 1621. Or was it on July 30, 1623? Or was it November 29, 1621? You get the idea, no one really knows. Others credit the settlers of Virginia's Jamestown with celebrating the first Thanksgiving as their version of England's ancient Harvest Home Festival, since there were no bowl games to watch. I don't think there were anyway.

For their first meal on the moon, astronauts Neil Armstrong and Edwin Aldrin ate roast turkey in foil packets.

And still another group of historians, who happened to be sitting in Newt's Olde Tyme Taverne swigging Rolling Rock last Sunday, swear that a guy named Morris Butterball started it all when he invited a few pilgrim friends over for beer and some sorta bird. Oh yeah, Pilgrims didn't drink

beer—in that case he probably gave 'em some more lime Jell-O mold and an extra drumstick.

President Abraham Lincoln, long before he went to the theater, proclaimed Thanksgiving a national holiday in 1863, supposedly as a response to a campaign organized by a feisty magazine editor Sara Joseph Hale.

Henry VIII was the first English king to like eating turkey.

From 1846–1863, Ms. Hale, the editor of *Godey's Lady Book*, a sort of *Ladies' Home Journal* of the 1800s, and the author of "Mary Had a Little Lamb," embarked on a campaign to turn Thanksgiving into a national holiday during which workers would not be required to go to work. Yeah Sara! Her campaign resulted in Lincoln's Thanksgiving proclamation—the first such proclamation of a national Thanksgiving holiday since 1789, when George W. proclaimed a National Day of Thanksgiving, a holiday which was dropped by subsequent presidents.

But after Lincoln's rescue of the day, Thanksgiving has been a national holiday, an American celebration of football and John Madden's six-legged turkeys, and a day in late November when we don't have to work. Thanks again, Sara and Abe.

In 1939, President Franklin Roosevelt moved Thanksgiving from the last Thursday to the third Thursday in November. He wanted to help businesses (malls, discount stores, and internet Web sites of the time) by lengthening the shopping period before Christmas. Today that shopping period seems only to have grown to run from July 5th until Christmas. In 1941, this unpopular move inspired Congress to permanently fix the date on the fourth Thursday of November.

Tom Turkey's real name: Meleagris gallopavo!

Through the years this date has been circled on turkey calendars all over the world, and those few turkeys lucky enough to see the following day's sunrise count themselves as really, really lucky. There are very few really, really lucky turkeys. It's a good thing that there has been a good supply of them, otherwise we'd have used them all up by about 1953.

In the year 2000, about 267 million turkeys were raised and it's estimated that 45 million of those turkeys were eaten at Thanksgiving, 22 million at Christmas and 19 million at Easter. That leaves a whopping 181 million birds that someone musta cooked, and I'll betcha a lot of them were cooked below the Mason-Dixon line.

In the early West, turkeys were trailed like cattle in "drives" to supply food where needed. One of the earliest turkey drives was over the Sierras from California to Carson City, Nevada. Hungry miners coughed up $5 apiece for the birds.

By the way, in case you haven't noticed, we all owe a heap of gratitude to those Southerners for discovering many of the foods that make up the best, tastiest part of American's only indigenous cooking style: **BARBECUE**.

Back on the cotton plantations, it seems white folks didn't want pig ribs and skin and shoulders, preferring hams, bacon, and tenderloins. So they let the slaves have the rest. Bad move all around, for the plantation owners anyway.

Result: Today's multi-billion dollar industry selling those same pig ribs, pork shoulders, and cracklings to a whole passel of folks, including a few plantation owners. Where would barbecue be today if those plantation honchos had liked ribs? But let's go back to the subject of our conversation, turkey. *No, not you*, we were talking about the bird. Turkey.

Big Bird, Sesame Street's oversized bird-of-some-sort, wears a costume made of turkey feathers.

For years this noble fowl has been roasted, broiled, smoked, diced, sliced, quartered, fricasseed, baked, braised, grilled, barbecued, and cooked in any one of a number of other ways. But leave it to those clever Southern folks again to discover the "Number One, Top Drawer, Most Flavorful, Most Delicious Way" ever invented to cook 'em.

Deep fat frying. The very thing our mothers, and now our wives, warn us about every day. Yup, taking a whole 12- to 22-pound bird and ceremoniously dunking him in $4\frac{1}{2}$–5 gallons of boiling oil, and in the time it normally takes you to get the oven up to temperature, he's done. And there you are pulling out the most golden, most moist, best tastin' turkey you've ever wrapped your teeth around.

Turkeys are high in protein, low in fat, and low in cholesterol.

We can't determine who first decided to deep fry whole turkeys, but we admire their intuition, and, let's call it what it is: "turkey pen savvy."

This simple process has exploded on the American culinary scene today with over 1,000,000 deep-frying units sold last year alone! Fer gosh sakes even Emeril, Rosie, Regis, and, oh yes, even "the Martha," is frying 'em on screen. Hey folks, that's a lotta oil, gas, birds, and greens. The kind of greens with presidential faces on the front, that is.

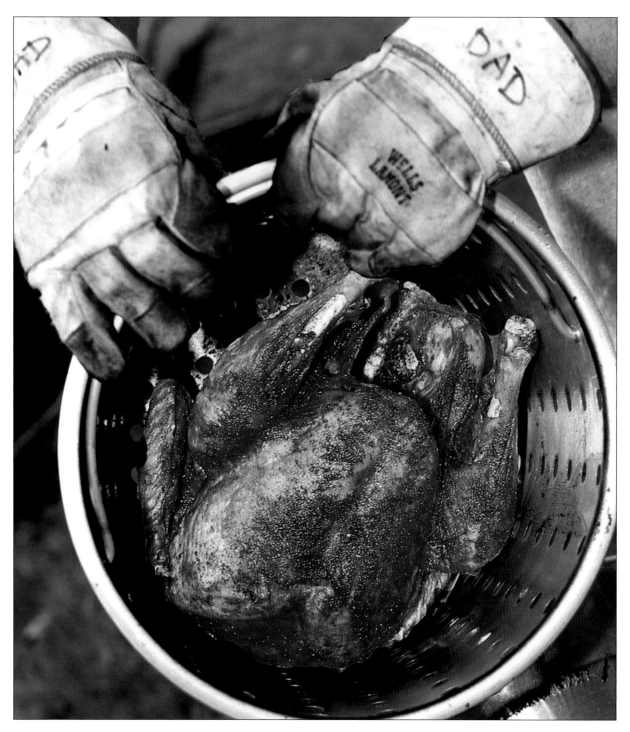

The biggest turkey on record was Tom Turkey Tyson, who weighed in at a hefty 85 pounds and was sold for £4,400 in 1989. In today's dollars, that's over 6,500 American greenbacks. Try fittin' him in your oven.

Deep-frying turkeys, which started as a Southern tradition, has in just the past 3 years boiled its way across the nation in a veritable frenzy. If *you* haven't fried a turkey, odds are you've tasted one someone else fried up, saw someone show Martha Stewart how to do it, or read in some foodie magazine the rapturous joys of deep-fried gobblers.

Purists say the deep-frying process seals the outside while the interior remains very juicy and the skin develops a crisp texture. Aficionados just say it tastes real goooood.

A 16-week-old turkey is called a fryer. A five- to seven-month-old turkey is called a young roaster and a yearling is a year old. Any turkey 15 months or older is called mature. A 17-month-old turkey is called "LUCKY."

Commercial caterers offer deep-fried turkey and restaurants feature the golden crisp bird during the holidays. At football stadium and baseball park tailgate parties, outdoor church suppers (do they still have these?) and neighborhood get-togethers, folks are setting up pots big enough to cook Volkswagens on their driveways, filling those pots with millions of gallons of precious oils, and lowering deceased birds into the stainless steel faster than a witch-dunking party in Salem, Mass.

Since most of us buy our turkey birds frozen: there are three, and only three, safe ways to defrost turkeys.

- In the refrigerator
- In cold water
- In the microwave

NEVER defrost a turkey on the kitchen counter, in front of a Duraflame log in your fireplace, or wrapped in foil and strapped to the engine of a '56 Ford truck. And please don't be like a certain Darwin Award Loser who tried to defrost a 24-pound bird in the dishwasher, then cooked it the next day. The *Salmonella* he contracted fried *him*.

In 2000, the average American ate 17.75 pounds of turkey.

To completely thaw a frozen 20-pound turkey the safest, most reliable, and slowest way, you'll need about five days in your nearest refrigerator.

Or if you want to speed things a tad, put "Tom," plastic wrapping and all, in a kitchen sink of COLD water in his see-though polystyrene suit, submerging him completely and changing the water every 30 minutes to be sure it stays cold. Depending on the size of the fowl, he/she could be thawed in as little as 2–3 hours, or it might take as long as 5–6 hours.

Turkeys have been on the planet for a mere 10 million years.

While turkey defrosted in the microwave is "OK," many say it's another open ticket to an intimate visit from either *Salmonella serotype Typhimurium* or *Salmonella serotype Enteritidis*, guests you'll be inviting to a sort of a modern day "last supper." Your last supper!

If thawed by this method, you best should cook Mr. Turkey like **right now**, because some hidden parts of him may well have become warm and provided a spa-like refuge for those salmonella twins during microwaving. Waiting to cook your bird for a few hours after microwave defrosting is like playing Russian roulette with maybe only 3 bullets in a six-chamber gun. Spin, click. Spin, click. Spin, **BLLLAAAM**!

Male turkeys (Toms) gobble,
females (hens) click when they speak.

The United States Department of Agriculture says that cooking Tommy Turkey the right way is as follows: "For whole turkeys the USDA recommends 180°F for thigh meat, 170°F for breast meat, and 165°F for stuffing, whether cooked alone or in the bird;" said temperature to be taken before or immediately after removing the turkey from the oven. But their own material also says anything over 160°F is safe.

Here is a highly technical graphic to indicate turkey "safe" temperatures:

Gobbling turkeys can be heard
a mile away on a quiet day.

I personally cook turkey to a thigh temperature of 170°–175°F. The breast meat will be a bit more moist, you're perfectly safe according to

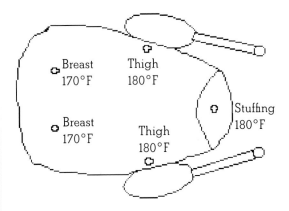

Breast 170°F   Thigh 180°F

Breast 170°F   Thigh 180°F   Stuffing 180°F

EVERY health source we contacted, and there are no known bacteria that can withstand such a high temperature.

Just about everyone says that the bird isn't the problem, but the stuffing can be a BIG PROBLEM. In fact, improperly cooked stuffing is thought to be the cause of most turkey food poisoning. But since deep-fried turkeys are NEVER stuffed, we're gonna happily go our own way and bring him out from the heat or hot oil when he's reached the safe 170°F temperature, letting him rest, covered in foil, for about 15–20 minutes so his internal juices retract back into the meat. Then we're gonna carve him up and eat 'im.

Ben Franklin thought the eagle of "bad moral
character" and actively sought to make the
turkey our national bird.

So we hope we jawed on long enough to make you hungry. In the words of my Aunt Rhoda: *"Let's go out to git ourselves a dad gurn turkey bird to fry up!"*

DEEP-FRYING A WHOLE TURKEY

First, before you do anything, follow the manufacturer's directions and check for gas leaks when you hook your burner up to a propane or natural gas line. And every time you turn it on, you should perform a simple test by putting soapy water on all joints to see if any gas leaks through the soap bubbles.

Where to cook? Do not set up your deep fryer on your lawn, unless you want to get rid of the section of lawn it'll be standing on. Unless you're a genius and don't spill any oil it'll kill your lawn quickern' a gallon of Roundup. And probably attract insects and nocturnal critters investigating that nice "oily-fatty" smell you've left there.

Best find a gravel driveway, or a section of garden where the dirt is nice and flat. If you have to set up on a cement driveway, at least put down a large piece of cardboard to sop up any spilled grease. Do not set up the deep fryer on your wooden deck. Let's see, boiling oil + propane gas flames + a wood surface. Nope.

NEVER, EVER fry indoors. And that means inside a garage as well. There have been quite a few houses that fried up along with the turkey in boiling oil when it caught on fire. Plus the smell of frying foods will linger for days, and you'd probably not want to have that scent lingering inside your garage, or most certainly not your kitchen.

Have an ABC fire extinguisher ready at hand. DO NOT USE WATER TO PUT OUT ANY OIL FIRE. Water and oil do not mix, so you could actu-ally make the problem worse by spreading the oil all over the place with water, plus hot oil virtually explodes when it's contacted by water. Use the pot lid or a large sheet of aluminum foil to smother flames, and if that isn't possible hit it with the extinguisher.

Have large potholders, or better yet, fireproof barbecuing gloves handy, too. Wear gloves, a long-sleeved shirt, long pants and close-toed shoes. Errant drops of 350°F grease can wreck havoc on exposed skin. Safety glasses or sunglasses aren't a bad idea as well.

Measure your oil properly. Don't guess. Spillage on a gas burner can be disastrous. Place the (un-breaded and/or un-marinated, please) turkey, roast, or other large items in the empty cooking pot, then pour in water until the food is covered by about two inches.

Carefully remove the food and mark with a pencil (they're graphite, not lead, these days, so you're safe) where the water level is now. Drain and thoroughly dry the pot.

Fill the pot with oil to that level only. Place the pot on the burner and light a fire to start the gas cooking. Use an appropriate deep fry thermometer with a very long probe to measure the temperature in the center of the oil. Bringing room temperature oil to 350°–375°F can take anywhere from 45 minutes to an hour.

Prepare the turkey at this time, injecting it, rubbing it inside and outside, marinating it, whatever. But DO NOT, I repeat DO NOT, STUFF THE TURKEY. Deep fry empty turkeys only. If you want

stuffing, mix it up, put it in foil or in a covered pot, and cook it in the kitchen oven.

If your turkey has one of those cute lil' pop-up temperature thingees, completely remove it, and, if you marinate it, remember to pat the turkey dry inside and out before you cook it. Liquid on the surface can cause face- or arm-scarring burns as the hot oil reacts to the liquid.

Do not heat oil beyond the recommended temperature for the kind of oil you're using. If the oil begins to smoke, it's too hot and may suddenly flame up. Then you have 4–5 gallons of boiling AND flaming oil. Not a good way to start your day.

Once the cooking oil has reached the right temperature, you're ready to fry up the bird. But again a few safety precautions are called for, unless,

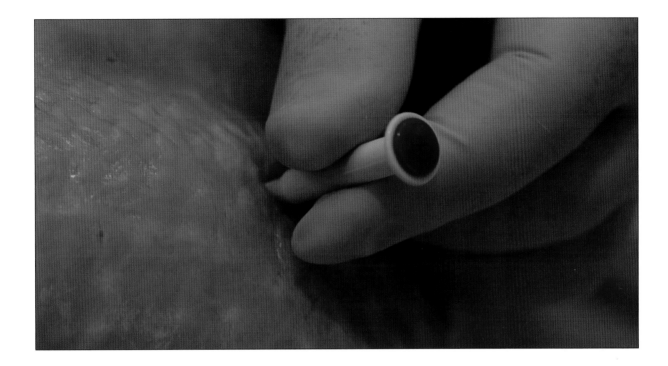

that is, you wish to get a costly, painful, and lengthy tour of your local hospital's burn ward.

Make sure the turkey is dry (inside and out) and at room temperature (or nearly so), and carefully place it in a turkey basket, or on a lifting rod or hook. In a cooking basket it doesn't matter which end is up, but on most lifting hooks the "arse end," or tail-end, of the turkey should be down. Make sure it's secure and won't fall off, splashing hot oil on you, when you try to lower it into the pot.

Before lowering the bird into the hot oil, have someone TURN OFF the gas under the pot. You do not want to spill oil onto a lit flame. Trust me on this. Carefully and slowly lower the turkey into the hot oil, lifting up and down several times as you lower it in so that the liquid can begin filling the inner cavities of the turkey. Don't rush it. Clip a deep-frying or candy thermometer to the edge of the pot so you can check the temperature anytime during cooking.

When the turkey is completely under the oil TURN THE GAS FLAME BACK ON and begin your timer. The oil temperature may also have fallen, so adjust the flame to go back up to 350°F and then adjust again to keep the temperature at that degree for the rest of the cooking time.

Whole turkeys require about 3–4 minutes per pound. That's right, 3–4 minutes. So a 20-pound turkey should be done in approximately 1 hour! That's a lot better than the standard 20 minutes per pound in a conventional oven. And we haven't even talked about the taste difference.

Immediately wash EVERYTHING that has touched, or been touched by, the raw turkey—including your hands, all implements, injectors, spoons, knives, countertops, and cutting boards—with hot soap and water. Rinse and dry. Saran Wrap has just come out with Cutting Sheets, a disposable plastic and paper sheet that you place on a counter or cutting board to handle turkeys, chickens, or other food. It keeps juices and fluids from touching the surface you're working on, and, after you're finished, you just throw it away.

While the turkey is merrily bubbling away in his hot oil bath you must NEVER LEAVE THE BURNER UNATTENDED. A pet, a neighbor's child, or one of your own may come by and investigate the fun thing you're doing in the backyard.

When the time has come to check the turkey you must again TURN OFF THE GAS before removing the bird from the hot oil.

If you can, have someone slowly and carefully lift the bird partially out of the oil so you can check the thigh and breast temperatures. If you're by yourself, set the turkey in a large pan on the table or counter while you take a meat thermometer and check the temperature at four different spots on Mr. Turkey.

First check **both** sides of the breast to make sure the temperature is 170°F. Then check **both** thighs to see if they are at 180°F. If so, the bird passes and is on the way to dinner.

If any of the temperatures are below those levels you must put the turkey back in the oil (following the same safety procedures as when you began to cook it) and cook until those temperatures are reached. Those are the safe guidelines laid down by the USDA and strictly followed by most other government health agencies, state and local health departments, turkey producers, restaurants, and deep-fry equipment manufacturers.

But since our turkey passed we'll finish up here. Set the bird upright in a large bowl, pot, or pan so the oil inside can drain out, and cover the entire bird loosely with aluminum foil. Let it rest for 10–15 minutes so that juices flow back from the outside

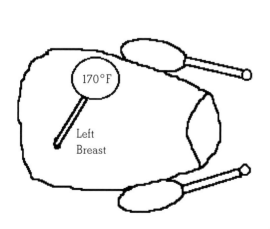

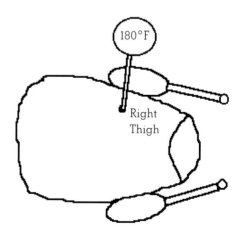

towards the center of the bird, while the oil flows into the container the bird is sittin' in.

Meanwhile, cover the oil and let it cool until it's reached the ambient temperature. Carefully using a filter pump, drain the oil back into its original container or into a large dark glass or plastic bottle. If you don't have a pump, carefully pour the oil in small batches through filtration into the same containers. Place used oil in a cool, dark spot until next time. You may wish to mark the date on the bottle of oil so you can keep track of how long the oil has been in use.

Carve and serve the turkey as usual. If you wish to avoid some of the cholesterol in the bird, remove the skin before you serve the meat. The bulk of any cholesterol in turkey, and all poultry, is in the skin, not the meat.

When finished the meal (fantastic, wasn't it?) cover and refrigerate any leftover meat, freezing what you can't eat in 2–3 days.

Compiled from safety and cooking guidelines from the FDA, the National Turkey Federation, the Washington State Farm Bureau & Department of Health, Foster Farms, Butterball Inc., and Cabela's online Web site.

TURKEY DEEP-FRYING CHECKLIST

- Heavy-duty portable propane burner
- Propane tank
- 26 to 40 quart stockpot
- Turkey holder (e.g., stand, cradle, vertical rack, or metal drain basket)
- Lowering mechanism (e.g., broom handle)
- Turkey
- Marinade
- Hypodermic meat injector
- Dry rub
- Peanut oil, 2–5 gallons for deep-frying pot
- Heavy oven mitts or leather gloves
- Long-sleeved shirt, long pants, closed shoes
- Large platter
- Paper bags
- Deep-frying thermometer (or candy thermometer)
- Aluminum foil
- Meat thermometer
- Paper towels
- An assistant
- A comfortable chair
- A chilled adult beverage
- A good book

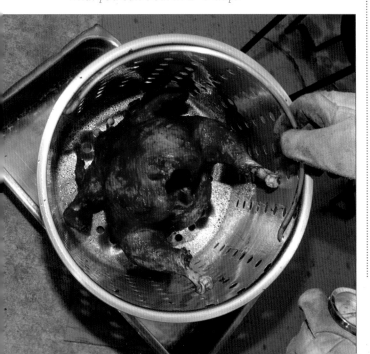

AH, THERE'S THE RUB!

Turkey, chicken, duck, & game hen rubs

The ingredients in the following rubs should be mixed together well, rubbed gently into the fresh poultry and left to dry-marinate for at least 4 hours, but preferably overnight. If you have leftover rub, discard it, but these amounts will cover a 20- to 24-pound bird with an adequate dusting.

White Knight Rub

¼ cup onion powder
¼ cup ground white pepper
1 tablespoon salt
2 tablespoons garlic powder
2 tablespoons granulated sugar

Curried Rub

¼ cup chili powder
1 teaspoon onion powder
1 teaspoon curry powder
1 teaspoon cumin
1 teaspoon garlic powder
1 teaspoon dry mustard
1 teaspoon white pepper
1 teaspoon oregano
2 teaspoons celery salt
1 teaspoon parsley flakes

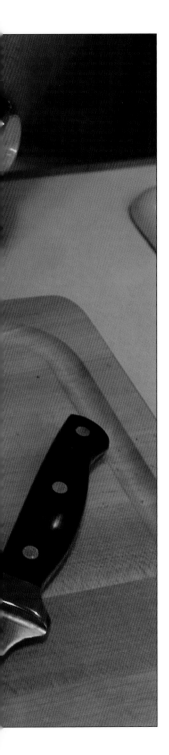

Bobtail Rub

3 tablespoons paprika, mild

2 teaspoons seasoned salt

2 teaspoons black pepper, freshly
    ground

2 teaspoons garlic powder

1 teaspoon cayenne, not too hot

1 teaspoon summer savory

1 teaspoon dry mustard

½ teaspoon chili powder

1 teaspoon thyme

1 teaspoon coriander

2 teaspoons green peppercorns

1 teaspoon allspice

Brandy's Rubbing powder

1 teaspoon garlic powder

1 tablespoon honey granules

½ teaspoon ground thyme

1 tablespoon lemon granules

1 tablespoon Worcestershire
    powder

1 teaspoon white sugar

Romanov Rub

1 garlic clove, crushed

10 allspice berries, crushed

½ teaspoon rosemary leaves, finely
    chopped

2 tablespoons olive oil

Casablanca Rub

2 tablespoons paprika

1 teaspoon salt

1 teaspoon sugar

½ teaspoon coarsely ground black
    pepper

½ teaspoon ground ginger

½ teaspoon ground cardamom

½ teaspoon ground cumin

½ teaspoon ground fenugreek

½ teaspoon ground cloves

¼ teaspoon ground cinnamon

¼ teaspoon ground allspice

¼ teaspoon cayenne pepper

Red River Rub

1 teaspoon cayenne pepper

1 teaspoon curry powder

1 teaspoon turmeric

1 teaspoon ground ginger

1 teaspoon ground cumin

1 tablespoon chili powder

1 tablespoon paprika

1 dash of nutmeg

STICKIN' IT TO THE TURKEY

239 MARINADES FOR YOU

Place the uncooked turkey in a pan. Load your favorite marinade into a hypodermic meat injector (like the Cajun Injector). Inject the marinade in multiple places on the turkey, especially through the breast, thighs, thick part of the wings, and legs. Marinate for 12–36 hours in the refrigerator.

There are about a zillion and three commercially bottled marinades available on the Internet, in grocery stores, in supermarkets, and in barbecue stores. Or, if you're cheap like me and like to mess around in the kitchen anyway, go to the following Web site and look over a list of 231 marinades you can do yourself: www.recipesource.com/side-dishes/marinades/index1.html

Put ingredients for each of the following marinades in a saucepan and heat until well mixed, cool and inject into turkeys, chicken, game hens, or IRS agents.

Alligator Marinade

    4 ounces liquid garlic *

    4 ounces liquid onion *

    4 ounces liquid celery *

    1 tablespoon ground red pepper

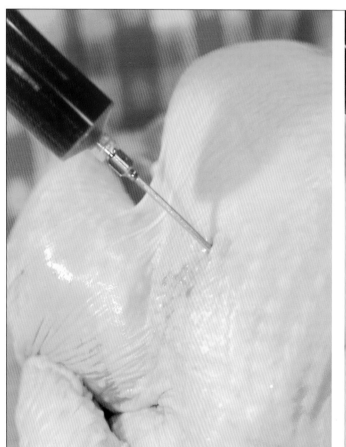
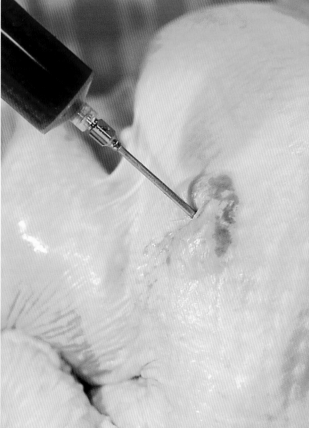

DEEP-FRYING A WHOLE TURKEY

2 tablespoons salt
2 tablespoons Louisiana Hot Sauce
1 ounce liquid crab boil * OR
1 tablespoon Old Bay Seasoning

Lemon Barbecue Marinade

½ cup lemon juice
¼ cup vegetable oil
½ teaspoon salt
1 teaspoon garlic powder
1 teaspoon onion powder
½ teaspoon black pepper
½ teaspoon ground thyme
1 teaspoon Worcestershire sauce

Mama Mia's Marinade

⅔ cup Wishbone Italian dressing
⅓ cup sherry, not cooking Sherry
2 teaspoons garlic powder
3 teaspoons Lemon pepper
1 teaspoon onion powder
2 teaspoons cayenne pepper

Tahiti Marinade

⅓ cup vinegar
¼ cup soy sauce
⅓ cup water
¼ cup fresh lime juice
¼ teaspoon garlic powder
⅛ teaspoon black pepper

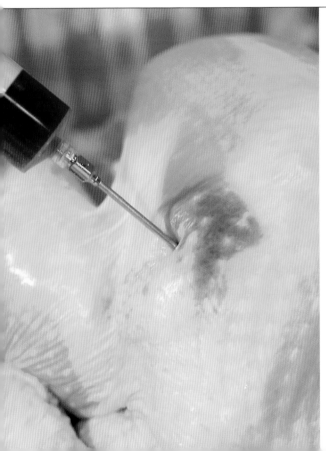 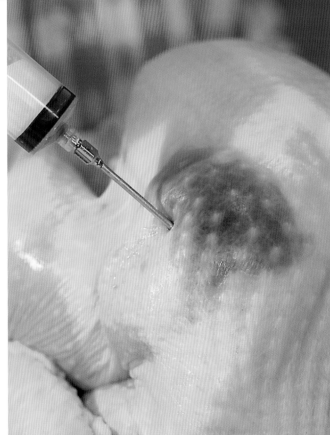

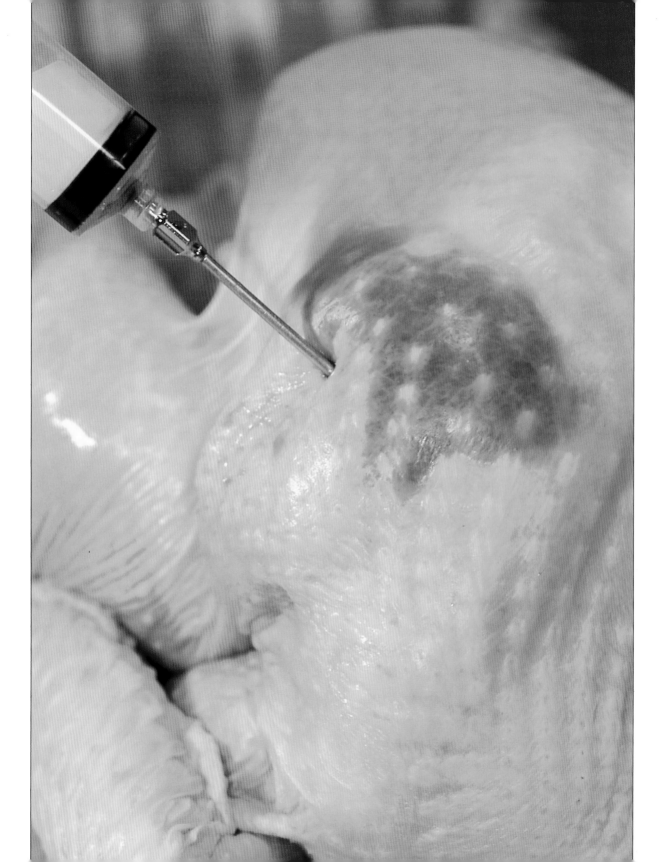

Pineapple Marinade

¼ cup soy sauce

½ cup pineapple juice

¼ cup rice wine vinegar

¼ cup brown sugar

¾ teaspoon garlic powder

Minute Marinade

1 bottle Italian vinaigrette

1 cup white wine

juice of 1 lemon

¼ cup melted butter

Popeye Marinade

2 tablespoons kosher salt

2 teaspoons garlic powder

2 teaspoons white pepper

1 teaspoon cayenne pepper

½ teaspoon onion powder

1 cup melted butter

Wild Turkey Marinade

⅓ cup red wine vinegar

⅓ cup olive oil

⅓ cup Wild Turkey whiskey

6 teaspoons garlic powder

5 teaspoons lemon pepper

5 teaspoons onion powder

2–3 teaspoons cayenne pepper

2 teaspoons paprika,

1 teaspoon cumin

2 teaspoons black pepper

1 teaspoon sugar

1 teaspoon powdered oregano

IMPORTANT RECIPE NOTE

UNLESS OTHERWISE SPECIFIED ALL THE FOLLOWING RECIPES ARE WRITTEN TO BE COOKED IN A DEEP FRYER THAT HOLDS FROM BETWEEN 2 TO 5 GALLONS (OR MORE, IN THE CASE OF TURKEYS, LARGE ROASTS, OR MULTIPLE FOWL COOKED AT THE SAME TIME).

THE SIZE OF THE POT YOU'RE COOKING IN DETERMINES THE AMOUNT OF OIL YOU NEED. REMEMBER TO PRE-MEASURE THE OIL FOR TURKEYS, ROASTS, LARGE FISH, OR OTHER FOWL BY PUTTING WHAT YOU WANT TO COOK IN THE POT, ADDING WATER UNTIL IT COVERS THE FOOD, REMOVING THE FOOD, AND THEN MEASURING AND MARKING THE NEW WATER LEVEL. YOU THEN DRAIN THE POT, DRY IT, AND THEN ADD THE CORRECT AMOUNT OF OIL.

MANY OF THESE RECIPES CAN ALSO BE ACCOMPLISHED IN A LARGE DUTCH OVEN WHICH WILL REQUIRE MUCH LESS OIL. A GOOD GUIDELINE IS TO USE 2" TO 3" OF OIL IN THESE COOKING POTS. BUT, AS IN THE LARGE POTS, BE CAREFUL NOT TO OVERFILL WITH OIL AND/OR FOOD TO PREVENT THE OIL FROM OVERFLOWING AND IGNITING ON THE GAS FLAME.

DEEP POT FRYER: 2 TO 5 **GALLONS** OF OIL

DUTCH OVEN: 2 TO 3 **INCHES** OF OIL

Appetizers

ACADIAN POPCORN

2 pounds raw crawfish tails (or small shrimp)

2 large eggs

1 cup dry white wine

½ cup cornmeal

½ cup flour

1 tablespoon fresh chives

1 garlic clove, minced

½ teaspoon thyme leaves

½ teaspoon chervil

½ teaspoon garlic salt

½ teaspoon black pepper

½ teaspoon cayenne pepper

½ teaspoon paprika

oil for deep-frying

Rinse the crawfish or shrimp in cold water, drain well, and set aside until needed. Whisk the eggs and wine in a small bowl, then refrigerate. In another small bowl, combine the cornmeal, flour, chives, garlic, thyme, chervil, salt, pepper, cayenne pepper, and paprika. Gradually whisk the dry ingredients into the egg mixture, blending well. Cover the resulting batter and then let it stand for 1–2 hours at room temperature.

Heat the oil in Dutch oven or deep-fryer to 375°F degrees on thermometer.

Dip the dry seafood into the batter and fry it in small batches for 2-3 minutes, turning it until golden brown throughout.

Remove the crawfish (or shrimp) with a slotted spoon and thoroughly drain it on several layers of paper towels. Serve it on a heated platter with your favorite dip.

Serves 4–6

BOB'S BEER-BATTERED ONION RINGS

3 large yellow onions
2 cups whole milk (or cream), chilled
2 cups ice water

BATTER:

1 ⅓ cups all-purpose flour
1 teaspoon salt
1 teaspoon dry mustard
¼ teaspoon freshly ground pepper
2 large eggs, at room temperature
2 tablespoons vegetable oil
¾ cup beer, at room temperature
dash of hot sauce
oil for deep-frying

Slice the onions crosswise about ½ inch thick and then carefully separate the slices into rings. (You should have about 8 cups.) Place the rings in a wide, shallow dish in as few layers as possible.

In a bowl, whisk together the milk and ice water. Pour the mixture evenly over the onions. Cover the dish with plastic wrap and refrigerate overnight. Very carefully turn the rings at least once to soak them evenly.

Also, the night before cooking, in a large bowl, whisk together the flour, salt, mustard, and pepper and set it aside. In a medium bowl, lightly beat the eggs; whisk in the vegetable oil, and then the beer and hot sauce, mixing well.

Make a well in the center of the flour mixture and pour in the egg mixture all at once. Whisk until the mixture is free of lumps. Cover and let it stand overnight.

The next day, cover two large cookie sheets with a double layer of paper towels. Using tongs, remove the onion rings from the milk mixture, shaking off the excess liquid, and let the rings drain on the towels. Pat the rings dry to remove all excess moisture.

In a deep fat fryer, heat the oil until it registers 375°F degrees on a deep fat frying thermometer.

Stir the batter and, working in batches, use the tongs to dip the onion rings in the batter, shaking off any excess. Quickly slide them into the hot oil. Fry the rings, turning occasionally with the tongs, until they are a deep golden brown on both sides. This will take about 4–5 minutes.

Using tongs, transfer the cooked onion rings from the oil to another paper towel-lined cookie sheet. Let them drain briefly, then serve while quite hot.

Serves 6

FRENCH
POTATO CURLS

4 pounds potatoes
salt, garlic salt, or celery salt to taste
¼ cup grated Parmesan cheese
oil for deep-frying

Scrub the potatoes thoroughly with a vegetable brush. Using a potato peeler, cut off long spirals of skin from the potatoes. In a large saucepan, cover the skins with very cold water and let them stand 30 minutes to 1 hour. Save the peeled potatoes in cold water and use them for another dish.

Drain and carefully pat the curls dry with paper towels.

Using tongs, drop the curls into a deep fryer heated to 390°F and fry them until golden brown and crisp, about 1 minute.

Using tongs, remove them from the fryer and drain on paper towels. Sprinkle them with salt, garlic salt, celery salt, or Parmesan cheese. Serve hot.

Serves 4–6

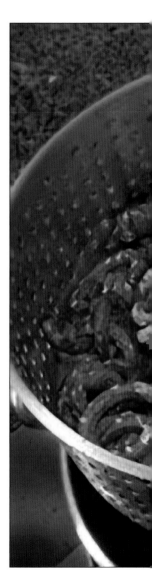

FRICKLES: FRIED PICKLES

2 cups flour
1 cup yellow cornmeal
2 tablespoons your favorite BBQ rub
¼ cup prepared yellow mustard
⅛ cup beer
hamburger dill slices

Heat deep fryer oil to 325°F.

In a wide flat pan, combine flour and cornmeal (50/50) and season the mixture with the BBQ rub. In a small bowl, make a slurry of mustard and beer.

Using your fingers, dip the pickle slices into the mustard mixture and then into the flour/cornmeal. Then, using tongs, take individual pickle slices and slip them into the hot oil. Deep fry at 325°F until the batter is browned. The pickles will float to the top of the oil when done.

Remove them from the hot oil with tongs and drain on absorbent paper towels on a shallow plate.

Serve these as an appetizer with an icy cold beer.

Serves 6–8

FRIED ONION BLOSSOMS

If there is a "Sold Only On TV" store in a mall near you, go and buy the onion blossom cutter, it works great and is a lot less work than doing each cut by hand.

DIP:

½ cup mayonnaise

½ cup sour cream

1 tablespoon chili powder

2 tablespoons ketchup

½ cup sour cream

1 ½ teaspoons McCormick Cajun seasoning

1 or 2 large sweet onions

BREADING:

1¼ cups flour

1 tablespoon McCormick Cajun seasoning

1 cup milk

oil for deep fat frying

In a small bowl, make the dip by combining mayonnaise, sour cream, ketchup, chili powder and 1½ teaspoons Cajun seasoning. Mix well and set aside.

Heat the oil in the fryer to 350°F.

Leaving the root end intact, peel the outer skin of the onion. Cut a small slice off the top. Starting at the top of the onion and on one side, make a cut downward toward the root end, stopping ½" from the bottom. Make additional cuts ⅛" from the first cut until there are cuts completely across the top of the onion. Turn the onion a quarter turn so the slices are horizontal to you. Repeat the cuts ⅛" apart from each other until there is a checkerboard pattern across the entire top of onion.

In a large bowl or resealable plastic bag, combine the flour and remaining Cajun seasonings. Pour the milk into a small bowl. Dip the onion in flour, then dip it into the milk, then back into the flour mixture. Fry the onion at 350°F for 5 minutes or until golden, turning once.

Using tongs, remove the onion from the oil; place it on a serving plate. With a spoon, remove the center of the fried onion blossom. Pour about ½ cup of the dip into the center of the blossom and serve it immediately.

Serves 4–6

GREEN DRAGONS WITH A GOLDEN HEART

2 cups whole jalapeno peppers
1 small bottle of Velveeta
1 cup all-purpose flour
1 teaspoon salt
1 teaspoon sugar
1 teaspoon ground black pepper
1 teaspoon chili powder
1 teaspoon garlic powder
2 eggs
1 cup beer
oil for frying

Take the contents of a small (8 oz.) bottle of Velveeta cheese and put them in a cloth pastry bag. Place the bag in a microwave and heat on medium heat for 1 to 1 ½ minutes until the cheese is very soft and runny. Set aside.

Cut a slit the entire length of the jalapeno and gently spread it apart. Take your pastry bag of warmed cheese and fill the inside of each jalapeno with cheese. Use just enough to fill the inside, being careful that the edges of the cut don't gap. You can also use cream cheese to which you've added yellow food coloring to make the filling a deep orange color.

Mix the flour, salt, sugar, pepper, chili powder, garlic powder, eggs, and beer together in a bowl. It should be quite thick. You may have to adjust by adding more flour to make a very thick paste which sticks to the pepper.

In a deep fryer, or large pot, heat the oil to 365°F.

Dip the stuffed jalapenos in the batter, and drain quickly. Using long tongs, place them immediately into the deep fryer. The jalapenos are fully cooked when they float to the surface of the oil. They should be golden brown and crispy. This should take about 1 to 2 minutes. Remove the jalapenos from the hot oil using tongs, drain on paper towels, and serve immediately.

Serves 4–6

LES JAMBES FRITES DE GRENOUILLE (YOU KNOW, D'EM FROG'S LEGS)

1 ½ to 2 pounds frog's legs
1 cup flour, in wide flat pan

BREADING:

½ cup flour
¼ cup seasoned bread crumbs
½ teaspoon lemon pepper
¼ teaspoon garlic powder
½ teaspoon green onion powder
½ teaspoon summer savory
dash of Louisiana Hot Sauce
1 teaspoon seasoned salt

BATTER:

4 large eggs
½ cup milk, or beer
⅓ cup blush wine, like Zinfandel
2 cups flour
¼ cup seasoned bread crumbs
1 teaspoon garlic salt

¼ teaspoon ground cumin
½ teaspoon onion powder
1 teaspoon Louisiana Hot sauce

In a large bowl, mix flour, bread crumbs, pepper, garlic powder, green onion powder, savory, hot sauce, and salt together. Stir well with a whisk or spoon to thoroughly mix all the ingredients. Set aside.

Using another large bowl, mix the eggs, milk (or beer), wine, flour, bread crumbs, salt, cumin, onion powder, and hot sauce and whisk until the batter is smooth and all ingredients are well incorporated.

Heat oil in deep fryer to 375°F.

Take frog legs and wash thoroughly. Then dip each frog leg into the pan of flour, rolling legs so they have a light coating of flour. Take each leg and dip into the batter, then, after briefly draining, into the breading, again rolling each leg so it's well covered with dry coating. Set on a plate while you finish with the rest of the legs.

Once you have finished coating all the legs, slip them (6 or 8 at a time) into the hot oil and fry till brown on all sides, about 3 minutes.

Remove from oil with slotted spoon or tongs and drain briefly on paper towels, serving on a heated platter over dirty rice.

Serves 2–4

MICKEY'S MOZZARELLA LOGS

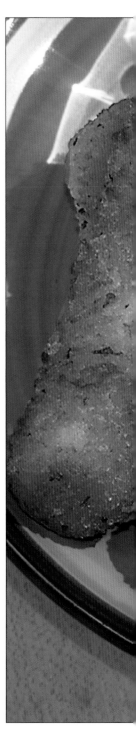

1 pound mozzarella cheese

1 cup all-purpose flour

⅓ cup cornstarch

3 eggs, beaten

¼ cup white wine

1 ½ cups Italian bread crumbs

1 teaspoon granulated garlic

½ teaspoon dried savory

½ teaspoon dried oregano

pinch red pepper

oil for deep-frying

Parmesan cheese to sprinkle

Heat the frying oil in a deep pot or Dutch oven to 350°F.

Slice the mozzarella lengthwise into ½" sections. Then cut each section in half so you have strips about 3" to 4" long by ½" wide.

In a medium bowl, mix the flour with the cornstarch and set the bowl aside. In another medium bowl, beat the eggs with a hand beater or whisk, add the white wine, whisk until incorporated, and set aside.

In a flat Pyrex pan or bowl, mix the bread crumbs, garlic, savory, basil, and red pepper, and set aside.

Roll the cheese logs in the flour, then dip in to the egg-wine mixture, and then roll in the bread crumb mixture.

Using tongs or a slotted spatula, carefully slip the logs (2 or 3 at a time) into the hot oil and fry them until golden brown. This will only take a few seconds, so you need to watch them closely.

Remove the logs with a spatula or tongs and drain them on paper towels. Serve them with marinara sauce or ranch dressing to dip. Sprinkle with parmesan cheese.

Serves 8

KOH SAMUI SPRING ROLLS

½ pound ground pork
  (or chicken)
1 tablespoon rice wine
1 ½ teaspoons arrowroot
¼ teaspoon black pepper
1 tablespoon sugar
1 tablespoon soy sauce
2 tablespoons vegetable oil
3 teaspoons salt
2 tablespoons minced fresh ginger

1 clove garlic, finely minced
1 cup onion, chopped
1 ½ pounds chopped Chinese
  cabbage
1 pound fresh bean sprouts
2 packages spring roll skins, about
  ¼ pound
1 egg, beaten
oil for deep-frying

Mix the pork or chicken with wine, arrowroot, pepper, sugar, and soy sauce in a large bowl and set aside.

Heat the oil in your fryer to 360°F.

In a medium saucepan on high heat, cook the pork mixture until all the pink color is gone, about 10–15 minutes. Add the salt, ginger, garlic, and onions; cook for 3–4 minutes.

Remove the mixture from the heat and drain in a colander for 5 minutes, saving the liquid, then spread the mixture on a cookie sheet to cool completely. Pour the reserved liquid into a pan, add the cabbage, and cook for 5 minutes over high, then remove from the heat, add the bean sprouts, and drain well in the colander. Add the pork mixture and stir well. Salt and pepper to taste.

To assemble the spring rolls, lay one spring roll skin on a cutting board with the point of the skin facing towards you. Place ⅓ cup of the filling on the skin and roll it up, folding the edges towards the middle. To seal the end, brush it with the beaten egg.

When all the rolls are assembled, put them in the deep fryer in small batches and fry until golden brown, about 3–5 minutes. Serve with hoisin or plum sauce.

Serves 6–8

N'ORLEANS SHRIMP CROQUETTES

1 pound shrimp

2 thin slices fresh ginger

1 clove garlic

1 large stalk celery, very crisp

1 teaspoon soy sauce

1 tablespoon oyster sauce

1 teaspoon fish sauce

3 tablespoons chicken broth

2 tablespoons cornstarch

1 teaspoon salt

oil for deep-frying

lettuce leaves for garnish

Heat deep fryer to 350°F.

Clean and devein the shrimp. Chop the shrimp very finely, almost into a paste. Mince the ginger and garlic and keep them separate from the shrimp. Slice the celery into ¼" pieces, removing strings as you cut.

In a small bowl, whisk together the soy sauce, oyster sauce, fish sauce, chicken broth, and 1 tablespoon of the cornstarch, and set aside.

In another bowl, combine the shrimp with half of the minced ginger and half of the minced garlic. Add the salt and the remaining tablespoon of cornstarch. Mix well, and with lightly moistened hands form this mixture into small croquettes about 2" long and 1" in diameter.

Heat the oil to 360°F and deep fry the shrimp croquettes 6 at a time, until they are golden brown, about 2–3 minutes. Remove the croquettes from the hot oil with tongs.

Drain the croquettes on paper towels and keep warm on a platter in an oven set on low heat.

Put 1 tablespoon of the hot oil from the deep fry pan in a saucepan or wok over high heat and stir fry the remaining ginger and garlic until it turns golden, about 1 minute, then add the celery and stir fry it on high heat for about for about 30 seconds. Add the reserved sauce mixture and stir until it thickens, about 2 to 3 minutes.

Cover a platter with lettuce leaves and arrange the croquettes on the leaves. Remove the sauce from the heat and pour over the croquettes. Serve hot.

Serves 8

SI SI CINNAMON SINNERS

Anne Callon, Jalisco, Mexico, says these are a "favorite way to spend a stormy evening during the winter."

10 8″ flour tortillas

SPICE MIX:

1 cup sugar
1 teaspoon ground cinnamon
¼ teaspoon ground nutmeg
¼ teaspoon ground allspice
oil for deep-frying

Heat deep-frying oil to 375°F.

In a large paper bag, combine sugar, cinnamon, allspice, and nutmeg, and set aside. Cut the tortillas into 3″ x 2″ strips.

Slip 4 to 5 strips into the hot oil at a time and fry them until golden brown on both sides, about 30 seconds per side. With a slotted spoon remove the strips, and drain them on paper towels.

While the strips are still warm, place them in the paper bag with the sugar-spice sugar mixture and shake gently to coat the strips evenly.

Remove the strips to a large bowl and serve immediately. You may also store them in an airtight container and serve cold.

Serves 6–8

SUGARED WALNUTS

3 cups water

2 cups walnuts, in large pieces (or pecans)

¼ cup brown sugar

salt to taste

1 tablespoon sugar

¼ teaspoon cinnamon

oil for frying

Bring 3 cups of water to a rolling boil in a large saucepan. Add the walnuts and blanch (boil) for 1 minute. Remove from the heat and rinse the nuts under hot water, quickly drain them, and then, in a small bowl, toss the walnuts with the brown sugar.

In Dutch oven, heat the oil to 350°F degrees.

With a slotted spoon, add half the walnuts to the oil. Fry, stirring constantly, 4–5 minutes or until golden. Repeat with the remaining nuts. Sprinkle with salt, sugar, and cinnamon and stir together.

Separate the pieces and cool them on an aluminum foil sheet. Serve warm.

Serves 4

Breads & Pastries

BUTTERMILK 'N BACON HUSH PUPPIES

2 cups yellow cornmeal

1 cup plain flour

¾ cup of white or yellow corn, if using frozen
    thaw completely

¾ teaspoon seasoned salt

½ teaspoon ground pepper

1 teaspoon baking powder

⅔ teaspoon baking soda

2 tablespoons brown sugar

2 eggs

⅛ cup bacon grease, melted

1 cup buttermilk

oil for deep-frying

Mix the cornmeal, flour, corn, salt, pepper, baking powder and soda, and sugar in a medium bowl. Add the eggs, bacon grease, and buttermilk. Stir it all up until the ingredients are thoroughly blended. Flour your hands and, using approximately 2 tablespoons of the thick batter, roll the hush puppies into small balls, 1" to 1½" in diameter.

Heat the oil to 350°F, then drop the hush puppies in the oil using a tablespoon. Allow them to brown on all sides, approximately 2 to 3 minutes.

They should begin floating when done, but if they don't, don't overcook them. They're ready when they're golden brown all over. Remove them from the oil with a slotted spoon or tongs, drain on paper towels and serve immediately.

Serves 6–8

BENGALI FRIED DOUGH WAFERS

1 ¼ cups all-purpose flour
1 ¼ cups whole wheat flour
1 teaspoon salt
1 teaspoon black pepper
1 cup ice water
oil for deep-frying

Heat the oil in a deep fry pot or Dutch oven until it reaches 375°F degrees.

In a deep bowl, combine the all-purpose and whole wheat flours, add salt and pepper, and stir the ingredients with a fork to mix them well. Make a depression in the center and add the ice water while stirring with fork. If the mix gets too dry, add more ice water, a teaspoon at a time. Stir until the dough clings together but isn't sticky.

Place the dough on a floured board and knead it for five minutes. Form it into a ball. Cut the ball into quarters then cut each of those quarters into 3 pieces. On a floured surface, form the dough into small balls, place them on a plate, cover, and let them rest for 30–40 minutes.

On a piece of floured wax paper, roll out each ball into wafer-thin rounds about 6–7 inches in diameter. Place them in a single layer on the wax paper, putting sheets of paper between each round, otherwise they'll stick together.

Gently slip each flour wafer into the hot oil. First it will sink and then it will rise to the top of the hot oil. When it rises back to the surface, use a wooden spoon or long tongs and hold the wafer under the surface until it puffs, about 20 seconds on each side until puffed and golden brown. Using tongs or a spatula, remove the wafers from the heat and drain on absorbent paper towels.

Serve with beans, curry dishes, or salsa dishes.

Serves 6–8

FRY D'AT BREAD MOMMA

3 cups all-purpose flour

2 teaspoons baking powder

1 teaspoon salt

1 tablespoon butter, or margarine

1 cup warm buttermilk

2 tablespoons melted butter, or margarine

1 teaspoon sugar

oil for deep-frying

Heat frying oil to 375°F in deep fryer pot.

In a large bowl, mix the flour, baking powder, and salt thoroughly. Add enough warm buttermilk ($^3/_4$ to 1 cup) to make a soft, easy to knead, dough. Knead on a floured board until the dough is very smooth and soft, but still elastic. Divide the dough into 6 to 8 balls and brush the tops with the melted butter. Cover the bread and let it stand 35 to 45 minutes.

Pat out each ball into a round, 5" or 6" in diameter, and ¼" thick. Fry dough rounds in deep fat until they rise to the surface, almost immediately. Then cook them until they are light brown on one side. Turn with a large spoon or spatula and brown them on the other side. Do not pierce the crust.

Remove the cooked bread from the hot oil with a slotted spoon and drain on paper towels. Serve hot.

Serves 6

GRAND MARNIER BEIGNETS

1 package dry yeast

4 tablespoons warm water

3 ½ cups flour

1 teaspoon salt

¼ cup sugar

1 teaspoon orange granules

1 ⅛ cups milk

3 eggs, beaten

¼ cup melted butter

⅛ cup Grand Marnier

1 cup powdered sugar

¼ cup lemon juice (optional)

oil for deep-frying

In a small bowl, dissolve the yeast in the warm water. Set bowl aside in a warm place for 15–20 minutes.

Heat the oil in a deep fryer to 375°F. In a large mixing bowl, combine the flour, salt, sugar, and orange granules, and mix well to ensure proper blending. Fold in the dissolved yeast, the milk, eggs, butter, and liqueur. Continue to blend until a smooth beignet dough is formed. Place the dough in a medium metal bowl, cover with a damp towel, and allow the dough to rise for one hour.

Remove the dough to a well-floured surface and roll out to approximately 1/4″ thickness. Cut it into rectangular shapes, 2″x 3″, and return them to a lightly floured pan. Cover the pan with a towel and allow the dough to rise for 35 to 45 minutes.

Deep fry the squares in the hot oil, turning once, until golden brown, about 3–4 minutes. Remove from the oil with a slotted spoon or basket strainer. Drain Beignets on a paper towel, and then dust generously with powdered sugar. You can also sprinkle with fresh lemon juice.

Serve warm with chicory coffee or other strong blend.

Serves 8–10

JACOB'S NAAN

Serve these Indian fried breads with curries and tandoori dishes.

½ cup milk

½ cup yogurt

½ teaspoon baking soda

1 teaspoon sugar

4 tablespoons butter, or margarine

2 eggs, lightly beaten

3 1-ounce pkgs. dry yeast

3 cups white all purpose flour

½ teaspoon salt

Heat frying oil to 375°F.

In a medium pan, over medium-low heat, warm the milk and stir in the yogurt until thoroughly mixed. Remove the pan from the heat. Add the baking soda, sugar, half of the butter, the eggs, and the dry yeast. Set aside.

In a large bowl, sift together the flour and the salt. Make a well in the flour and gradually add the warmed milk-yogurt mixture, stirring it into the flour as you pour.

Knead the flour for 10 to 15 minutes until it becomes smooth and elastic. Brush the dough with some of the remaining butter. Cover dough with a warm, damp cloth and set the naan aside in a warm place for 3 hours, or until the dough has risen to twice its size.

Preheat your oven broiler to high.

Knead the dough again for a few minutes, having first floured both hands, and divide the dough into 8 equal-sized pieces. On a floured surface use a heavy rolling to roll each piece into an 8" to 10" pancake. Cover the pancakes with a warm, damp, cloth for another 20 minutes.

Slide naans, one at a time, into the hot oil and cook them until they start to brown and float on the surface, about 30 seconds to 1 minute.

Remove cooked naans and drain them on paper towels. Brush one side of each naan with the remaining butter and the other side with warm water. Place the warm-water side of the naans under your oven broiler for about 2 minutes.

Serves 8

MR. DOBB'S COWBOY BREAD

½ cup boiling water

¾ cup cold milk

1 teaspoon white sugar

1 ½ teaspoons active dry yeast

1 egg, beaten

2 tablespoons butter, melted and cooled

¼ teaspoon salt

¼ teaspoon ground nutmeg

4 cups all-purpose flour

In a large bowl, stir together the water, milk, and sugar. Sprinkle the yeast over the top, and let the mixture stand for 5 minutes to dissolve the yeast.

Stir the egg and butter into the yeast mixture, then stir in the salt, nutmeg, and 2 cups of the flour.

Mix until everything is well blended. Mix in the remaining flour, ½ cup at a time until the dough pulls away from the side of the bowl. Turn the dough out onto a floured surface, and knead for 10 FULL minutes. Place the dough into a greased bowl in a warm spot in the kitchen, and let it rise until doubled in size, about 30 minutes.

Divide the dough into 8 balls, and let them rest for another 20 minutes. Roll each ball flat out to 8 to 10 inches in diameter.

Using a slotted spoon or spatula, gently slip each of the pieces of bread into the hot oil and cook from 30 to 60 seconds on each side, or until light to medium brown spots appear.

Remove from heat with a spoon or spatula. Keep them covered with a damp cloth, or store in a Ziploc plastic bag until serving time. Serve warm with plenty of real butter and homemade preserves.

Serves 4–8

NARGISI PURI

2 eggs, boiled, peeled & mashed
2 medium potatoes; boiled, peeled & mashed
1 tablespoon fresh mint
1 green chili, seeded & finely chopped
2 teaspoons salt
1 ½ cups flour, all-purpose
2 tablespoons vegetable oil
2 tablespoons warm water for kneading
oil for deep-frying

Heat deep fryer to 350°F.

In a small bowl, knead together the mashed eggs, potatoes, mint, chili, and 1 teaspoon salt and divide the mixture into 8 portions. In a separate bowl, sieve the flour and the remaining salt into the mixture, then add 2 tablespoons vegetable oil. Mix well, approximately 5 minutes. Slowly add the warm water. Knead to a soft dough. Divide the dough into 8 equal parts and shape them into balls. Roll each ball out to about 2″. Place one portion of egg mixture in center of each ball. Fold it over and pinch the ends. Now roll out each into a round Puri, 4″ in diameter. Do not make them too thin or the stuffing will come out.

Deep fry in a deep pot fryer one or two at a time until the pastries turn golden, about 2–3 minutes.

Serve hot with plain yogurt.

Serves 6–8

NAVAJO FRY BREAD

4 cups all-purpose flour
1 tablespoon double-acting baking powder
1 teaspoon salt
1 teaspoon sugar
1 ½ cups water
1 cup vegetable shortening
½ cup honey
powdered sugar, for sprinkling

Heat fryer to 350°F.

In a medium bowl, mix the flour, baking powder, salt, and sugar. Add the water and mix well until it reaches a dough-like consistency. Knead the dough on a floured board till it becomes elastic, then let it rest for 10 minutes, covered with a moist towel.

On a floured surface, roll out the dough till it is ½" thick. Cut it into 4" circles. Deep fry at 370°F in vegetable shortening till the bread is golden brown, about 2–3 minutes, then drain the cooked fry breads on paper towels.

Drizzle with the honey, or sprinkle with the powdered sugar and serve.

Serves 6–8

PARISIAN BREAKFAST BREAD

4 eggs

¾ cup cream

¾ cup whole milk

¼ cup granulated sugar

1 teaspoon vanilla extract

1 teaspoon lemon zest

1 tablespoon sugar

6 slices of stale French, Italian, or Challah bread,
    in ¼"-thick slices

powdered sugar for sprinkling

cinnamon for sprinkling

nutmeg for sprinkling

In a large bowl, beat the eggs, cream, milk, 1 tablespoon sugar, vanilla, and lemon zest until well mixed and a frothy yellow color.

Place the bread slices in a flat Pyrex dish and pour the egg mixture over the slices, turning them over carefully after 5 minutes to coat both sides. Refrigerate, covered, overnight.

Heat 2" of oil in a Dutch oven, or deep pan, to 375°F.

Carefully slide each slice of bread into the hot oil using a large spatula. Fry the bread, 1 or 2 at a time, for 1½ minutes each side. Lift from the oil with a slotted spoon or spatula, and drain on a paper towel. Keep the bread warm on a plate in the oven, on low heat, until all the slices are done.

Serve the bread warm. Sprinkle the bread with powdered sugar, cinnamon, and nutmeg.

Serves 4–6

PORTUGUESE FRIED BREAD

2 cups all-purpose flour
3 teaspoons baking powder
½ teaspoon salt
2 tablespoons sugar
¾ cup milk
oil for frying
¼ cup sugar
2 tablespoons cinnamon
honey

Heat frying oil to 350°F.

Whisk together the flour, baking powder, salt, and sugar. Add the milk, and knead until it reaches a dough-like, smooth consistency.

Divide the resulting dough into 16–20 balls. Pat them out on a flat, floured surface to ½" thick each.

Fry the dough pieces, 1 or 2 at a time, in a deep fryer, or in 1" to 2" hot oil in a Dutch oven, browning both sides, about 3–4 minutes.

Remove from oil with slotted spoon or spatula, drain on paper towels, and serve warm.

In a small bowl, mix the cinnamon and sugar to sprinkle over warm breads. You may also drizzle honey over the cooked fry breads.

Serves 8–10

SOPHIA'S SOPAIPILLAS

These are delicious drizzled with honey or stuffed with refried beans, chili, chopped onion, grated cheese, and guacamole.

4 cups all-purpose flour, sifted
1 ½ teaspoons salt
1 teaspoon baking powder
1 tablespoon lard (or butter)
1 package active dry yeast
¼ cup warm water at 115°F degrees
1 ¼ cups milk
vegetable oil for deep-frying

In a medium saucepan, scald the milk, then set pan off the heat and let it cool to room temperature.

In a medium bowl, combine the flour, salt, and baking powder, and mix in 1 tablespoon lard or butter. Cut into the flour with a pastry cutter or fork. In another medium bowl, dissolve the yeast in the warm water. Add the cooled, scalded milk.

Make a well in the center of the flour mixture and add the yeast-water-milk liquid slowly, working it into the dough, until the dough is firm and springy and holds its shape, about 2 to 3 minutes. Cover dough with a damp towel or invert the bowl over the dough and set aside at room temperature for about 10 minutes.

Heat oil to 350°F degrees in a deep fryer.

Roll ¼ of the dough to ¼" thickness, then cut it into 3" triangles; do not re-roll any of the dough. Continue with remaining dough, ¼ at a time, until all the dough is cut into triangles.

To assure puffing, slightly stretch each piece of dough before lowering it into the fat. Cover the cut dough with a towel as you fry the Sopaipillas, a few at a time, in hot oil.

They should puff up and become hollow very soon after being slipped into the fat. Hold each piece of dough under the surface with tongs or a slotted spoon until dough puffs, about 30 seconds. Remove the Sopaipillas with a slotted spoon and drain on paper towels.

Serves 6–8

SANTA MARIA DEEP-FRIED BREAKFAST BISCUITS

If you're in a hurry you can use frozen, pre-packaged biscuits from the grocery store.

1 ½ packages dry yeast
½ cup warm water, 105°F
2 cups milk, room temperature
⅛ cup sugar
½ cup shortening, or lard
3 teaspoons salt
4 ½ cups all-purpose flour

Heat deep-frying oil to 350°F.

In a small bowl, add the yeast to warm water and let the mixture sit for 5 minutes. Add the milk, sugar, shortening, salt, and flour, and mix well with large spoon. When mixed, roll the dough 1" thick on a floured board and using a biscuit or cookie cutter cut the dough into 2" circles. Set dough aside and let biscuits rise by about 50%.

Slip the biscuits into the hot oil, 3 to 4 at a time, and fry them until they puff up and are golden on both sides. Remove them from the hot oil with a slotted spoon and drain biscuits on paper towels. Serve hot.

Makes 36–40 biscuits

VIRGIN ISLANDS JOHNNY CAKES

2 cups flour
2 tablespoons baking powder
1 teaspoon sugar
1 teaspoon salt
2 tablespoons shortening (Crisco works well)
⅓ cup warm water
oil for deep fat frying

Combine the flour, baking powder, sugar, and salt in a mixing bowl. Add the shortening. Stir until the mixture resembles coarse crumbs. Add the water. Stir until a stiff but smooth dough forms. Knead thoroughly, but lightly, until any lumps are gone. Place the dough on a floured board, cover it with a damp towel, and let it rest for 30 minutes.

Heat oil to 350°F degrees in deep fryer or Dutch oven. Roll the pieces of dough into balls and flatten them. Fry both sides until golden, about 3 to 4 minutes. Remove them from the oil with a slotted spoon or spatula, drain on paper towels, and serve hot.

Serves 6

Pork & Beef

ANNE'S JALISCO MEAT PIES WITH CHEESE

2 cups all-purpose flour

2 teaspoons baking powder

1 teaspoon salt

6 teaspoons cold shortening

8 tablespoons ice water

MEAT FILLING:

1 pound lean ground pork

¼ pound chopped olives stuffed with pimentos

1 teaspoon salt

2 tablespoons recaito (Goya Recaito in Mexican food stores)

½ teaspoon dried oregano

½ teaspoon black pepper

4 ounces tomato sauce

1 beaten egg

grated cheddar cheese

Heat deep fryer to 375°F.

Sift the flour into a bowl with the baking powder and salt. Add the shortening to the flour mixture and, with a dough blender or a fork, blend together working very fast.

Add the water 1 tablespoon at a time, mixing well. Flour a flat surface and place the dough on top of it. Using your palms, knead the dough very well until smooth. Form it into a ball and cover with a moist towel to sit for 30 minutes.

While you are waiting, start your meat filling:

Brown the ground pork in a medium skillet over high heat, add all of the other filling ingredients, except the grated cheese, stir well and cook for 15 to 20 minutes, until the meat is well browned. Remove the filling from the heat and let it cool.

Roll out the chilled dough with your hands into a long roll on a floured board. The roll should be about 14" long. Cut off small 1" to 1 ½" lengths and roll out these pieces of dough so they're very thin, about ⅛" in thickness.

Put some of the grated cheese and meat in the middle and fold over one side so that the cheese and meat are covered. Brush the edges with beaten egg and seal them with a fork, making sure there are no openings. Put each pork turnover you make on a floured piece of aluminum foil while you finish the other pastries.

Fry them in oil at 375°F degrees. Once you put them into the oil, start basting them with the hot oil immediately, or hold them gently under the hot oil, and they will begin to inflate. Fry until golden brown on both sides, about 3 to 4 minutes. Drain them on absorbent towels.

Serve very warm.

Serves 6–8

BAXTER'S CHICKEN-FRIED STEAK

1 pound top round steak, trimmed
 (½"- thick), cut in 4 pieces
1 cup buttermilk
1 teaspoon Louisiana hot sauce
1 cup all-purpose flour
1 teaspoon salt, plus salt to taste

1 tablespoon paprika
1 tablespoon garlic granules
½ teaspoon freshly ground pepper
2 cups whole milk
3 tablespoons flour
oil for deep-frying

Using the flat side of a wooden kitchen mallet, pound the steaks to ¼" thick. Set them aside.

In a cast-iron Dutch oven, pour in oil to a depth of 2" to 3" and heat the oil to 375°F.

In a small bowl, mix the buttermilk and hot sauce. In a medium bowl, combine the flour, 1 teaspoon salt, paprika, garlic, and the pepper and mix well.

Put the steaks in a paper bag and add 2–3 tablespoons of the seasoned flour and shake to coat each piece of meat. Then dip each steak in the buttermilk, then back into the bag with the flour mixture a second time.

Reserve 1½ tablespoons of the remaining flour mixture and set it aside.

Deep fry the steaks, two at a time, turning once, until golden brown on both sides, about 2½ to 3 minutes. Using a slotted spatula, or a long pair of tongs, transfer the meat to a warm oven to keep them warm while making the gravy.

Carefully drain off all but 1½ tablespoons of the oil from the Dutch oven, it's still very hot. Over a very low flame (low heat), whisk in the reserved flour mixture and cook for 1 minute. Whisk in the milk and bring it to a simmer for approximately 3 minutes.

Remove gravy from the heat and season with salt and pepper to taste. Serve the steak immediately, with the gravy on the side in a sauce dish.

Serves 4

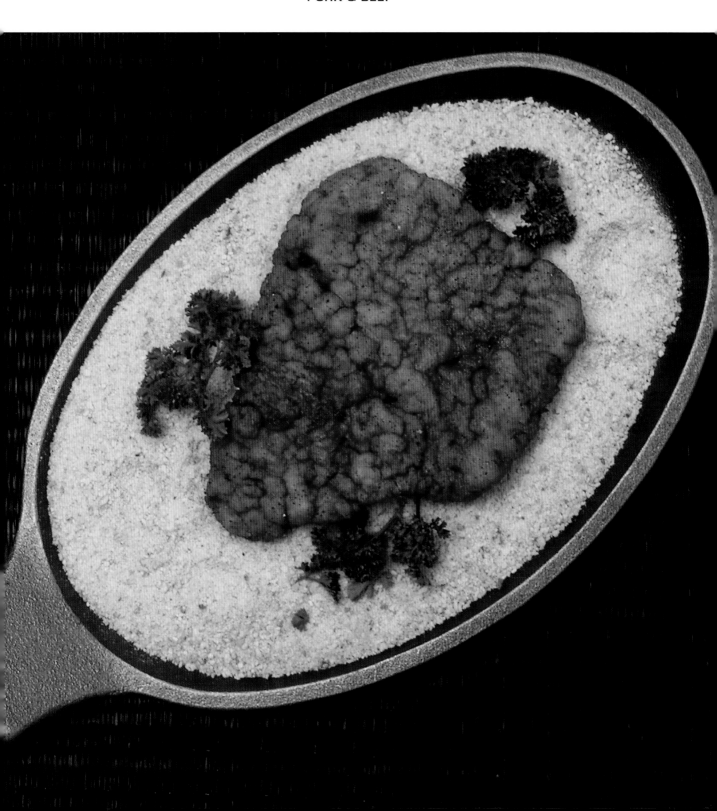

DEEP-FRIED SPARERIBS

Whole slab pork ribs

RUB:

¼ cup granulated garlic

¼ cup paprika

¼ cup seasoned salt

¼ cup lemon pepper

2 cups flour

2 cups yellow corn meal

oil for deep fryer

Hold slab of ribs in a horizontal position and, using a sharp knife, separate one rib from the slab by cutting right up against the bone. You now have a rib with meat on one side still attached to the slab. Take your knife and move over one rib so that you cut up against the second rib, thereby giving you a rib with meat on both sides. You get less rib bones, but each one has more meat on each side. Repeat on the remaining ribs, leaving all of the meat on one side of every second rib.

In a small bowl, mix the rub well. Take the individual ribs and rub them with half of the rib mix. Let the seasoned ribs sit at room temperature for about an hour. (The ribs will become tacky.)

Mix the flour and the cornmeal. Add the rest of the rub ingredients and roll each rib into flour/corn meal mixture.

Heat the oil to 350°F in a 28- or 30-quart. frying pot. Place the ribs in a frying basket, TURN OFF THE GAS, and slowly lower the ribs into the hot oil.

TURN ON THE GAS and cook the ribs for approximately 15 minutes or until they are a golden brown.

TURN OFF THE GAS while you slowly remove the frying basket of ribs from the pot.

Drain on paper towels, and then serve with your favorite barbecue sauce on the side.

Serves 2–4

FRY-GRILLED PORK TENDERLOIN

3 pounds pork tenderloin
salt and pepper to taste

RUB:

1 teaspoon dried rosemary
1 teaspoon garlic powder
1 teaspoon seasoned salt
1 teaspoon lemon pepper
1 teaspoon ground ginger
1 teaspoon chili powder

MARINADE:

12 ounces black cherry soda
⅔ cup packed brown sugar
½ cup soy sauce
¼ cup lemon juice
⅔ cup plum jam
½ stick butter
oil for deep-frying

Heat oil to 400°F in a deep fryer or Dutch oven. Salt and pepper the tenderloin and deep fry it in hot oil for 3 minutes until well browned. Remove, drain, and cool to room temperature.

In a medium bowl, combine the rub ingredients and rub mixture into the warm meat. Refrigerate the tenderloin overnight.

Combine the soda, brown sugar, soy sauce, lemon juice, and jam in a small saucepan over low heat; cook until well combined. Whisk in the butter to finish the marinade.

Bring the meat to room temperature, place in a Ziploc bag and pour ⅓ of the marinade over the meat. Seal the bag and marinate for 1 to 2 hours in the refrigerator. Turn once or twice during that time. Drain the meat and discard the marinade. Bring the meat to room temperature.

Heat barbecue grill to high heat 500° to 600°F.

Oil the grate on the grill, bring the grill to high temperature and place the tenderloin on the grill. Immediately turn heat down to medium and grill for 10–15 minutes, turning 2–3 times. Baste often with half of the reserved marinade, making sure the meat doesn't burn due to the sugar content of marinade. Boil the remaining marinade in a medium saucepan for 10 minutes, remove from heat, cool, and put in a sauce boat.

Cover the meat in foil and let it rest for 5 minutes. Slice into 1/4" thick medallions and serve with the hot marinade sauce.

Serves 6–8

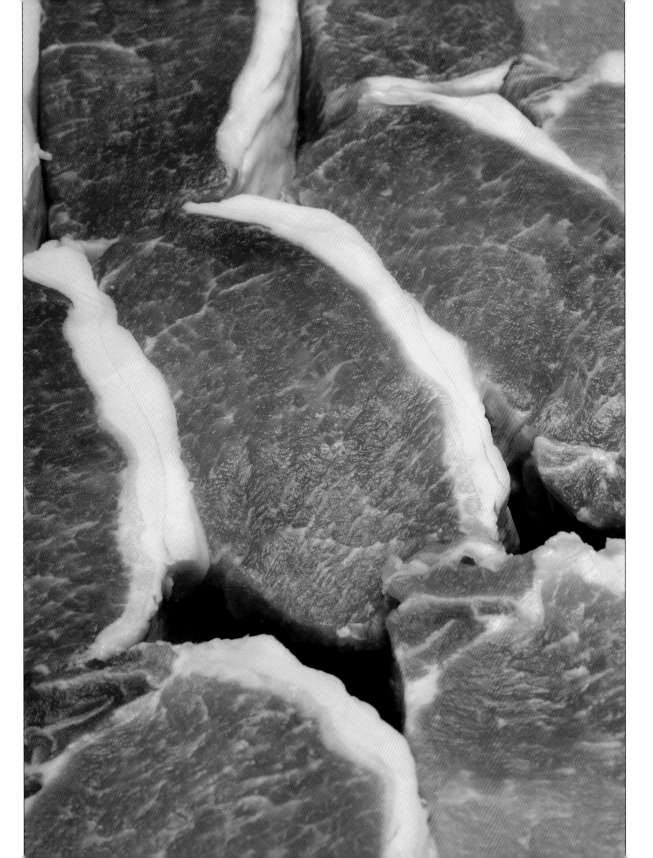

MAYUMI'S TEMPURA PORK CHOPS

Serve with teriyaki sauce or 2 cups apple sauce spiced with 1 teaspoon rice vinegar, ¼ teaspoon cloves, and ½ teaspoon cinnamon.

4 pork chops
½ teaspoon salt
¼ teaspoon pepper
¼ cup flour
1 egg, beaten
½ cup bread crumbs
oil for frying

Heat oil to 360°F.

Cut several vertical slits into the fat along the edges of the pork chops, to prevent chops from curling while cooking. Sprinkle salt and pepper on the chops.

Put the flour in a plastic bag, add salt and pepper, and add one pork chop, shaking the bag until it's covered. Dip both sides of the floured pork chop in beaten egg in a shallow dish. Coat the chop with bread crumbs in another flat dish, and pat the chop to firmly set the crumb coating.

In 2 to 3 inches of hot oil in a Dutch oven fry the pork chops for a few minutes until one side turns brown, about 2–3 minutes. Turn the chop over and cook the other side until brown.

Remove the chops from the hot oil with tongs and put them on a paper towel to drain.

Serves 4

NIGHTSHADE RANCH COW PIES

CRUST:

4 cups self-rising flour

½ teaspoon salt

½ cup Crisco

2 eggs

1 ½ cups milk

MEAT MIX:

3 tablespoons vegetable oil

1 large onion, chopped

½ red or yellow bell pepper, chopped

1 ½ pounds ground chuck

1 ½ pounds pork sausage

1 tablespoon Louisiana hot sauce

⅛ teaspoon cayenne pepper

½ teaspoon garlic salt

1 clove garlic, chopped

1 teaspoon chopped cilantro

½ teaspoon brown sugar

1 teaspoon Worcestershire sauce

oil for deep-frying

To make the crust, blend the salt into the flour in a medium bowl, add the eggs, and then cut in the Crisco and blend with a fork until the flour looks slightly crumbly. Then form the dough into a ball and refrigerate for at least 1 hour.

Dump the dough onto a clean floured counter top or cutting board and roll to ¼" thickness. Fold the dough onto itself twice, and then roll out again, this time to ⅛" thickness. Cut out 6" circles, then re-roll the leftover dough and cut another batch of circles. Repeat until all dough is used. Refrigerate the circles, covered with waxed paper or plastic wrap, while you make the filling.

Heat the oil and the flour together in a heavy, large cast-iron skillet. Cook over medium heat, stirring constantly, to make a medium-brown roux. Add the onions when the color is right, and sauté the onions until they begin to brown slightly, then add the bell peppers and cook for another 2 to 3 minutes.

Add the ground chuck and pork, hot sauce, cayenne and salt, cooking the mixture until there is no pink left in any of the meat. Remove meat from heat and drain it in a large colander.

Heat a large skillet to which you've added 1 teaspoon of oil, over high heat. A drop of water dropped in the skillet sizzles when the right temperature is reached. Add the garlic, cilantro, brown sugar, and Worcestershire, cooking for 1–2 minutes until the garlic just starts to color, then add the drained meat mixture and cook for another eight to ten minutes or so, stirring now and then to keep the meat from clumping, until the meat is well browned.

Transfer the meat mixture to a clean metal colander to drain and cool for a few minutes. Put the meat in a container, cover, and refrigerate overnight. The next day, bring it to room temperature to make the pies.

On a floured surface, take a dough circle and place a generous serving-spoon-sized amount of filling onto one half of a dough circle. Moisten the edge of the circle with a little water and fold the unfilled half over into a half-moon, then press down the edges with a fork to seal them so that a pocket is formed around the filling.

Heat oil in deep fryer to 350°F.

Fry 1–3 pies at a time, maximum, until golden brown, about 4 to 5 minutes, making sure the temperature has returned to 350°F as you start each batch.

Drain the pies and sprinkle them with paprika. Serve them warm or hot.

Makes 18–24 servings

JAMBON SAUCE

1 18-ounce jar crabapple jelly
1 18-ounce jar mint jelly
4 tablespoons prepared mustard
½ teaspoon cinnamon
½ teaspoon nutmeg
1 tablespoon black pepper
dash of Louisiana Jalapeno Hot Sauce

In a small saucepan, combine all ingredients and heat over medium heat until well combined and smooth. Remove pan from heat and pour sauce into glass bottle. Cover and chill until ready to serve. Warm to room temperature and put in saucepan to serve alongside ham balls.

Makes 4 cups

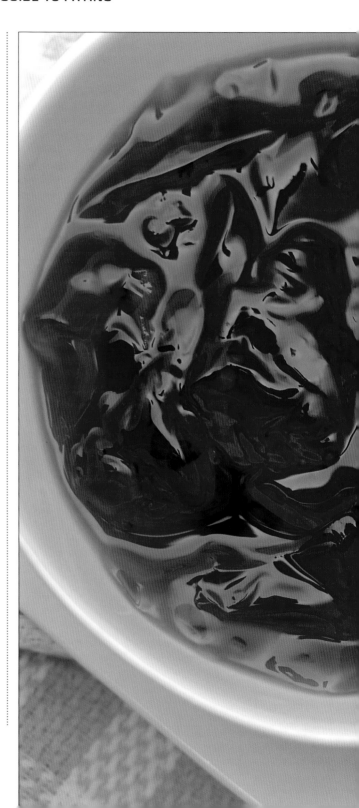

OLD SMOKEY'S HAM BALLS WITH JAMBON SAUCE

2 smoked pork chops, finely chopped, about ½ pound

1 pound smoked ham, finely chopped

1 pound ground pork, or turkey

2 cups seasoned breadcrumbs

3 large eggs, beaten

1 large sweet onion, minced

¼ cup finely chopped green onions, green tops only

1 teaspoon chopped parsley

1 tablespoon brown sugar, firmly packed

2 teaspoons dry mustard

1 teaspoon seasoned salt

pepper to taste

½ cup cream, or half and half

1 tablespoon Steen's Cane Syrup, or molasses

dash of Louisiana Hot Sauce

oil for deep-frying

In a large bowl, combine the pork chops, ham, ground pork, bread crumbs, eggs, onion, green onions, parsley, brown sugar, mustard, salt, and pepper. Then add the cream, cane syrup, and hot sauce. With a large spoon, mix well and refrigerate, in a covered bowl, for at least 20 minutes.

Remove from the refrigerator and, using your hands, shape into 1″ to 2″ balls. When all the mixture has been used up, you should have close to 40 ham balls. Refrigerate in a covered dish for a minimum of one hour. Longer is better, up to 4 hours.

Heat the oil in the deep fryer to 375°F.

Remove the meat from refrigerator and, using large slotted spoon, transfer the ham balls to the hot oil, frying in batches, until the balls are crispy brown and cooked through, about 3 to 4 minutes.

Drain them on paper towels. Serve the ham balls on a bed of lettuce on a large platter. Accompany with Jambon Sauce (see below).

Serves 8–10

PEDERNALES RIVER SHORT RIBS OF BEEF

2 to 2 ½ pounds beef short ribs

3 green onions, chopped in 1" pieces

2 garlic cloves, mashed

½ teaspoon minced fresh ginger root

3 tablespoons Steen's Cane Syrup

2 teaspoons brown sugar

1 teaspoon seasoned salt

2 tablespoons olive oil

3 bottles beer

BATTER:

2 eggs, beaten

4 tablespoons cornstarch

1 teaspoon garlic salt

1 teaspoon black pepper

dash of Louisiana Hot Sauce

Heat frying oil to 375°F in Dutch oven or deep pot fryer.

With a sharp meat cleaver, chop the ribs into 2" lengths. Place them in a large stockpot or Dutch oven. Add the green onions, garlic, ginger, cane syrup, brown sugar, salt, olive oil, and beer to the pot.

If ribs are not covered, add cold water until they are completely under liquid. Bring the ribs to a boil over high heat, then lower the heat, cover the pot, and simmer for 1 hour.

Drain the ribs in a colander, reserving 1 cup of the cooking liquid. Let the ribs cool.

Beat the eggs lightly and blend with the cornstarch to a make a smooth batter. Thin slightly with some of the reserved beef stock. Add the salt, pepper, and hot sauce. Using tongs, dip the ribs into the batter to coat them completely.

Using long tongs add ribs, 2 to 3 at a time, to the hot oil and deep fry them until they are golden on both sides.

Remove the ribs with tongs, drain them on paper towels, and serve on a heated platter with your favorite BBQ sauce on the side.

Serves 4–6

PITCHFORK STEAKS

WARNING: A PITCHFORK has three tines which are slightly curved, a MANURE fork has four tines that are almost straight. Be careful which one you buy to cook on. "Pitchfork steaks" sounds exotic and fun, "Manure Fork steaks" sounds, well, less than appetizing.

4 1-pound rib-eye steaks
4 tablespoons olive oil
2 tablespoons McCormick's Montreal Steak
    seasoning
4 pats butter
oil for deep-frying

Heat oil in deep fryer to 385°F.

Rub each of the steaks with 1 tablespoon. of olive oil, then sprinkle generously with the Montreal steak seasoning.

Take a brand new pitchfork and skewer all 4 steaks on the tines.

Dip the pitchfork in the hot oil for 2 ½ minutes (medium rare) to 3 ½ minutes (medium).

Remove the steaks to sizzling platters and serve them immediately. Put a pat of butter on each steak on the platter and let it melt into the meat and mingle with the juices.

Serves 4

STATE FAIR CORN DOGS

1 cup flour
1 cup cornmeal
1 tablespoon sugar
1 tablespoon baking powder
1 teaspoon salt
dash of pepper
2 eggs
1 cup milk
¼ cup vegetable oil
1 pound hot dogs
oil for deep-frying

In a large bowl, mix together the flour, cornmeal, sugar, baking powder, salt, and pepper, and stir the ingredients together. In a medium bowl, beat the eggs with milk and add ¼ cup oil. Pour this mixture into the flour mixture and whisk them together until the batter is smooth. Let the batter sit for 20 minutes to firm it up; it should be very thick and coat the dogs evenly.

Heat oil in the deep fryer to 360°F.

Insert a popsicle stick into each hot dog. Using the stick as a handle, dip each hot dog into the batter and turn to coat it evenly. Fry several corn dogs at a time, making sure they don't stick together, until golden, about 3–5 minutes. Drain on paper towels. Serve with yellow mustard and ketchup.

Serves 4–8

YOU-AIN'T-GONNA-BELIEVE-THIS PRIME RIB

1 6- to 8-pound prime rib
2 teaspoons kosher salt
2 teaspoons citrus-flavored black pepper
2 teaspoons chopped fresh rosemary
5 garlic cloves, slivered
oil for deep-frying
sprig of fresh parsley (or rosemary) for garnish

The night before you plan to serve your prime rib, mix the salt, pepper, and rosemary and rub the meat with it liberally. Using a small knife, make shallow cuts all over the roast, then insert slivers of garlic. Cover the meat and place it in the refrigerator overnight.

Remove the roast from the refrigerator and bring it to room temperature (1–1 ½ hours).

Heat 3 gallons of peanut oil to 365°F in a turkey pot with hook and stand or boiling basket.

Turn off the gas, then slowly lower the prime rib into the oil. You can expect the oil to drop in temperature quickly, probably down to approximately 330°F. Turn the gas back on and heat up the burner to bring the temperature back up to 365°F, then level off the heat as you reach the correct temperature.

Cook the prime rib for 3 minutes per pound of weight for medium-rare (18–24 minutes), 4 minutes per pound for medium (24–32 minutes).

Using the frying basket or tongs, carefully remove the prime rib from the hot oil and let it rest, covered with aluminum foil, for 10–15 minutes on a broiling pan.

Slice and serve the meat on a heated platter garnished with sprigs of fresh parsley, rosemary, and deep-fried onions (see next page).

Serves 8–10

FRIED ONIONS

1 dozen boiling onions, peeled with roots
    trimmed (about 1″ to 1 ½″)
brown sugar for sprinkling
fresh ground pepper to taste
pinch of garlic salt

After the prime rib (see previous page) has been removed, use a slotted spoon to remove any large particles floating in the oil.

Then, using a slotted spoon, slip the onions into the 365°F oil and cook till brown, 2–3 minutes, turning with a wooden spoon to evenly cook.

Remove the onions from the pan with a slotted spoon and quickly drain them on paper towels, then transfer the onions to a small saucepan over medium-high heat and sprinkle with brown sugar, salt, and pepper to taste. Cook them briefly until the sugar starts to caramelize, about 4 to 5 minutes, then serve the onions alongside prime rib or beef roast.

Serves 8–10

Poultry

BEER-BATTERED CHICKEN

Serve these strips with honey mustard beer dip, which you make by mixing ¼ cup honey mustard and ¼ cup beer until smooth.

1 ½ pounds boneless, skinless chicken breast halves
1 ½ cups all-purpose flour
1 teaspoon baking powder
2 eggs, beaten
½ cup beer
1 teaspoon salt
½ teaspoon cayenne pepper
1 tablespoon summer savory
oil for frying

Rinse the chicken and slice it into 1″ strips. In a medium bowl, stir together 1 cup flour and baking powder. Mix in the beaten eggs and beer, set aside. Place remaining ½ cup flour in a small bowl or brown paper bag, add salt, cayenne pepper, and savory, and shake to mix well.

Heat oil in a Dutch oven or deep fryer to 375°F.

Drop the chicken strips into the bag and shake well to coat evenly. Dip the floured strips into the batter. Fry a few at a time in hot oil in a Dutch oven or deep fryer, turning once, until the coating is golden brown on both sides, abut 4 to 5 minutes.

Remove the strips from the hot oil with tongs or a slotted spoon and keep them warm on platter in an oven set on lowest setting until serving.

Serves 4–6

BUTTERMILK FRIED CHICKEN

2 cups buttermilk
1 ½ teaspoons salt
½ teaspoon freshly ground black pepper
3 pounds frying chicken pieces
1 cup all-purpose flour
oil for deep-frying

Combine the buttermilk with half the salt and pepper. Put the chicken in a Ziploc plastic bag and pour the mixture over the chicken pieces, turn all the pieces to coat them well, and refrigerate them overnight.

Heat oil in a Dutch oven or deep fryer to 365°F.

In a medium bowl, mix the flour and other half of the salt and pepper. Drain the marinade from the chicken pieces and, using either a paper bag or shallow dish, coat the chicken pieces in the flour mixture, shake off the excess, and place the pieces in a single layer on a sheet of waxed paper.

Carefully add the chicken pieces to the hot oil and cook for 5 to 7 minutes, with the lid on. Remove the lid, turn the chicken, and cook the pieces for another 5 to 7 minutes. Remove the lid and cook them for another 8 to 10 minutes, until the skin is crispy.

Remove the chicken pieces with tongs, and drain the pieces on paper towels. Serve immediately on a heated platter.

Serves 4–6

CAJUN DEEP-FRIED TURKEY

MARINADE:

1 cup Italian dressing, important that it be strained

¼ cup Louisiana hot sauce

2 tablespoons liquid smoke

¼ cup garlic powder

2 tablespoons seasoned salt

1 defrosted 10- to 12- pound turkey

1 cup Cajun seasoning, or favorite rub mix

oil for deep-frying

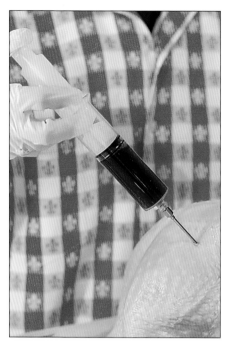

Mix the marinade ingredients together and add enough water to make 1 quart of marinade.

Remove the giblets from the turkey, then wash it and pat it dry, especially inside the cavity. Using a food syringe, inject 8 ounces of the marinade into each breast and each thigh and leg. Rub inside the cavity and all of the outside of the bird with the Cajun seasoning or rub mix. Marinate the turkey in the refrigerator for at least 24 hours, but if you can, marinate for 2–3 days.

When you're ready to cook, heat the oil in a deep fryer to 360°F, using a deep-frying thermometer to check the temperature.

Place the bird on a turkey basket or holder. SHUT OFF THE GAS FLAME. Slowly lower the basket into the oil, stopping, turning, and lifting it slightly as needed to prevent splattering, until the bird is submerged. TURN THE GAS BACK ON AND RE-LIGHT.

Cook 3–4 minutes per pound, (30–40 minutes), or until temperature in thigh is 160°F and breast is 180°F.

When finished TURN THE GAS OFF.

Then slowly lift the turkey out of the pot and drain it on paper towels, covered with foil, for about 20 minutes.

Carve the turkey and enjoy.

Serves 8–10

CHICKEN IN A BLANKET

PARCHMENT-WRAPPED CHICKEN

4 scallions, green tops only

2 large chicken breasts

4 teaspoons minced ginger

2 teaspoons rice wine

2 teaspoons soy sauce

1 teaspoon salt

¼ teaspoon white pepper

1 teaspoon sugar

2 teaspoons oil

1 cup teriyaki or hoisin sauce, for dipping

24 squares (6" x 6") parchment paper

oil for deep-frying

Shred the scallions lengthwise and then cut them into 1 ½" lengths, then cut the chicken breasts into strips ½" wide by 1 ½" in length.

Put the fresh, minced ginger in a garlic press and squeeze out 1 teaspoon of ginger juice. In a medium bowl, combine the ginger juice with the wine, scallions, soy sauce, salt, pepper, and sugar to make a marinade for the chicken strips. Let the chicken marinate at room temperature in a covered container for at least 30 minutes.

Place a square of parchment in front of you, with one corner toward you. Rub a little oil in the center of the paper and place 1 tablespoon-sized piece of chicken and some scallion on the paper horizontally, well below the center of the angled square.

Fold the lower corner up to cover the meat, then fold the left corner over to the right and the right corner over to left, to make a small envelope. Fold the top corner down and tuck it in securely. Repeat using all parchment paper squares, using the rest of the chicken and scallions.

In a deep fryer, heat the oil to 375°F.

Deep fry 2 or 3 envelopes at a time in the hot oil for 1 minute on each side. Remove them with a slotted spoon or a spatula, and drain them on paper towels.

Serve them with the teriyaki or hoisin sauce on the side for dipping. Each person gets two to three envelopes put on their plate and everyone opens their envelopes as the meal begins.

Serves 10–12

COXHINA, COXHINA

Portuguese fried drumstick dumplings

3 chicken breasts, skinned and boneless
½ medium onion, chopped
2 cloves of garlic, finely chopped
2 cubes chicken bouillon
6 tablespoons butter
1 ½ teaspoons salt
½ teaspoon lemon pepper
4 cups water
1 small green onion, chopped
¼ cup chopped fresh parsley
3 cups all-purpose flour
1 8-ounce package cream cheese
2 egg whites
bread crumbs

In a large microwave-safe bowl, cook the chicken breast, onion, garlic, chicken bouillon, butter, salt, pepper, and water in a microwave oven on high. The chicken should be cooked through in 10 minutes.

Remove the chicken breasts and finely chop them. For color, add the parsley and green onions.

In a medium saucepan boil, 3 cups of the remaining broth for 10 minutes. Add the flour and stir vigorously for about 1 minute until it becomes a moist dough. Take the dough out of the pan and cool it to a warm temperature. Knead it until it becomes smooth and all flour lumps are gone, about 10 minutes.

Heat deep fryer to 350°F.

Flatten the dough to ¼" thickness with a rolling pin and cut 2 ½"–3 ½" size circles with a biscuit cutter or drinking glass. Place the dough in your palm, add 1 teaspoon full of cream cheese and 1 teaspoon of the chicken filling.

Vary the amount of ingredients according to the size of the dough circle you cut so that you can close the dough with the filling staying inside. Knead any unused scraps of the dough and roll them again, cutting more circles until all the dough is used.

Fold and close the dough in the shape of a drumstick ("coxinha" means a little chickendrum stick in Portuguese).

Brush the filled dough generously with egg whites and roll them over bread crumbs until they are coated.

Deep fry the Coxhina for about 8 minutes or until golden brown. Remove from hot oil with slotted spoon or spatula. Drain on paper towels and serve hot.

Serves 6–8

CURRIED TURKEY BREAST

RUB:

1 tablespoon salt

1 tablespoon paprika

1 tablespoon brown sugar

1 tablespoon poultry seasoning

1 tablespoon pepper

1 tablespoon ground cumin

2 tablespoons curry powder, mild

1 tablespoon thyme

1 3- to 5-pound turkey breast

Heat the oil in fryer or Dutch oven to 350°F.

In a small bowl, mix all of the rub ingredients and stir to blend completely. Gently massage the rub mixture into the turkey breast, covering all surfaces. Let it rest at room temperature for 1 to 2 hours.

Place the turkey in a deep fryer basket and SLOWLY lower the bird into the oil with tongs or frying basket.

Breast should cook for 7 minutes per pound of meat and add 5 minutes to get a total cook time. (3 pounds of turkey breast X 7 minutes per pound = 21 minutes + 5 additional minutes = 26 minutes total cook time).

When the cooking time is complete, turn the gas OFF and remove the breast slowly to avoid spilling the oil. Use tongs or turkey lifter to remove the bird if you cooked it in a Dutch oven. Let the breast sit for 10 minutes covered in foil.

Cool and serve.

Serves 6–8

DEEP-FRIED LEMON CORNISH HENS

2 1 ½-pound Cornish game hens
¼ cup fresh rosemary leaves
2 tablespoons lemon pepper
2 tablespoons dried lemon zest granules
1 teaspoon garlic powder
2 teaspoons salt
oil for deep-frying
lemon wedges for serving

Rinse, clean, and wipe dry the game hens, patting them inside and out with a paper towel.

In a small bowl, mix rosemary, lemon pepper, lemon zest granules, garlic, and salt. Reserve half of the mixture and set it aside. Rub the other half into the hens, sprinkling them inside too. Let them stand, covered, at room temperature for 1 hour.

Heat the oil in a deep fryer or Dutch oven to 375°F. Carefully put the Cornish hens into the hot oil and deep fry until golden brown, about 12 minutes.

To check for doneness, use a slotted spoon or tongs to carefully remove the hen from the pot and insert an instant-read thermometer in the thickest part of the thigh, not touching the bone—it should read 180°F.

Transfer the hens to a wire rack and let them rest, covered, for 5 minutes. Serve them whole, or use a cleaver to split them in half lengthwise. Sprinkle each hen with the reserved spice/herb mixture and serve.

Serves 2–4

GARLIC CHICKEN GOLF BALLS

2 pounds ground chicken (or pork)
½ teaspoon citrus pepper
½ teaspoon salt
½ teaspoon poultry seasoning
2 tablespoons cornstarch
2 tablespoons soy sauce

3 EGG WHITES:

½ teaspoon freshly grated ginger
2 tablespoons Marsala wine (or use a favorite sherry)
4 cloves garlic, crushed

BATTER:

1 cup cornstarch
1 cup flour
oil for deep-frying

Heat oil to 375°F in Dutch oven or deep-frying pot.

In a large bowl thoroughly mix the chicken with the pepper, salt, poultry seasoning, and egg whites. Let the mixture rest for 10 minutes, covered with plastic. With your hands, form the chicken mixture into golf ball-sized balls and set them on waxed paper or aluminum foil.

Mix the cornstarch with the flour and roll each ball in this mixture to coat evenly.

Slip the balls into the oil and cook until they float and are golden brown, about 5 minutes. Remove with a slotted spoon and drain on paper towels. Serve warm.

Serves 8

GOLD NUGGETS

½ cup flour

1 ½ teaspoon garlic salt

1 teaspoon paprika

1 teaspoon sage

1 teaspoon onion powder

½ teaspoon white pepper

½ teaspoon poultry seasoning

½ cup water

1 egg, lightly beaten

3 whole boneless chicken breasts, skinned and cut
into 1 ½" by 1 ½" nuggets

oil for deep-frying

1 bunch fresh parsley for garnish

grated Parmesan cheese for garnish

paprika for garnish

Heat the oil to 375°F in a deep fryer.

Combine the flour and seasonings in a medium glass
bowl, add the water and egg, and stir well to make
a smooth batter.

Dip the chicken pieces into the batter, allowing any
excess to drain. Slip 3 to 4 pieces at a time into the hot
oil, and fry until crisp—about 2 to 4 minutes. Drain the
nuggets well on paper towels, then transfer the chicken
to a warm platter garnished with fresh parsley. Sprinkle
with grated Parmesan cheese and paprika and serve.

Serves 6

KRISPY CREAMED QUAIL

These are super served with crisp potato pancakes and stir-fried veggies.

8–12 young farm-raised quail
2 cups coarsely chopped sweet onions
2 cups cream
1 teaspoon Louisiana hot sauce
4 cups all purpose flour
2 tablespoons onion salt
1 teaspoon cayenne pepper
1 tablespoon brown sugar
2 teaspoons coarse-ground black pepper
oil for deep-frying

Wash the quail thoroughly under cold running water, making sure you remove all the fat that may not have been removed during processing. Then set them in a 1- or 2-quart Ziploc sealable bag. Prick the quail all over with a sharp fork or small knife so the marinade can invade the insides and flavor the meat.

At this point sprinkle the chopped onions over the birds and immediately mix them in well so that the quail pick up the flavor of the onions. Close bag and let them sit at room temperature for ½ hour, rotating the bag often.

In a small saucepan bowl, blend together the cream and the hot sauce and pour it into the bag, over the quail and onions, to form a marinade. Let the birds marinate overnight, or for at least 4 hours.

Just before you are ready to cook them, heat the oil to 350°F degrees in a deep fryer or deep Dutch oven.

Pour the flour into a large baking pan and add the salt, cayenne, sugar, and black pepper. Mix thoroughly.

Remove each quail from the marinade, and then liberally dust them in the coating mix, shake off the excess flour, and carefully, using tongs, slip them into the hot oil.

Fry quail for about 10–12 minutes. The outside should be golden brown and crispy, and the inside should be light, moist, and delicately tender from the cream-onion marinade. Discard the marinade and the onions.

Serve immediately.

Serves 8–12

LEMON CHICKEN STRIPS

2 pounds boneless chicken breast

BATTER:

½ cup flour

½ cup cornstarch

¼ teaspoon garlic salt

½ teaspoon double acting baking powder

½ teaspoon vegetable oil

SAUCE:

2 large lemons

3 tablespoons brown sugar

½ cup white wine

1 teaspoon cornstarch

2 teaspoons water

parsley sprigs for garnish

oil for deep-frying

Heat oil to 350°F in Dutch oven or deep-frying pot.

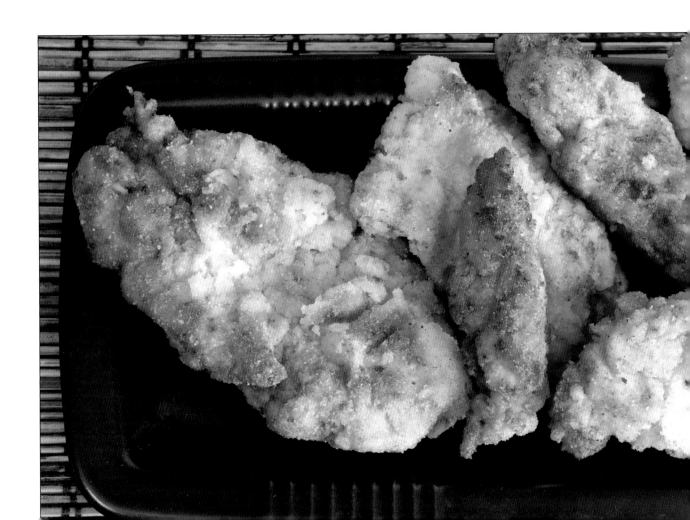

Cut the boneless chicken breast into strips about 3" long by ½" wide. Place them in a shallow bowl and cover with plastic wrap and set aside.

In a medium bowl, mix the flour, cornstarch, baking powder, salt, and oil with a large spoon, and stir until smooth.

Cut one lemon into ¼" slices and set aside. Squeeze the juice from the second lemon into a small bowl, add the sugar and white wine, and stir well. Set aside.

In a small cup, mix the cornstarch and 2 teaspoons water. Stir to mix completely. Set aside.

Dip each piece of chicken into the batter and let the excess drip back into the bowl.

Deep fry the chicken in small batches of 10–12 pieces. The chicken strips should brown up nicely in 4–5 minutes. Make sure they don't stick together.

Remove the finished strips from the oil with a slotted spoon and drain them on paper towels.

Cook the lemon sauce by pouring the lemon-sugar-wine mixture into a small saucepan and bringing the liquid to a boil over high heat. Add the cornstarch-water mixture and stir until the mixture is thickened.

Place the drained chicken pieces on a colorful plate, add lemon slices for garnish, and sprinkle with parsley. Serve lemon sauce on the side.

Serves 2–4

PERTH DEEP-FRIED WINGS

16 chicken wings
8 tablespoons soy sauce
7 tablespoons oyster sauce
8 tablespoons sweet sherry
3 tablespoons lime juice
salt and pepper to taste
1 cup all-purpose flour
1 cup corn flour
oil for deep-frying

Heat deep fryer to 375°F.

Place the chicken wings in a non-porous glass dish, Ziploc plastic bag, or stainless steel bowl. Using a knife, poke holes in the wings to allow the marinade to penetrate into the meat.

In a small bowl, mix the soy sauce, oyster sauce, sherry, lime juice, salt, and pepper, and pour the mixture over the chicken. Cover the dish, or seal the bag, and refrigerate it for 12 to 24 hours.

Remove the chicken from the marinade, disposing of the remaining marinade. Mix the flours together in a shallow dish or bowl and toss the wings in this mixture until well coated on all sides.

Heat the oil in a deep fryer. Cook the wings until they are crispy brown, cooked through, and the juices run clear, about 4–5 minutes.

Drain on paper towels and serve.

Serves 8

SPICY FRIED GOBBLER STRIPS

3- to 4-pound turkey breast

MARINADE:

1 tablespoon Heinz chili sauce

1 teaspoon Mexene chili powder

2 teaspoons rice wine

2 teaspoons soy sauce

1 teaspoon powdered ginger

1 tablespoon finely chopped green onions

1 teaspoon brown sugar

FLOUR COATING:

⅔ cup flour

1 teaspoon paprika

1 tablespoon poultry seasoning

Heat the frying oil to 350°F in a Dutch oven or deep-frying pot.

On a cutting board, with a sharp knife, cut the turkey breast into strips, 3" long by 1" wide.

In a large bowl, mix the chili sauce, chili powder, rice wine, soy sauce, ginger, green onions, and brown sugar together, and pour the mixture over the turkey strips. Stir well to make sure each strip is covered.

Marinate the strips for 1 hour at room temperature. While the turkey is marinating, mix the flour, paprika, and poultry seasoning in a wide, flat bowl or pan and set aside.

Remove the strips from the marinade and drain well over the bowl. Heat the remaining marinade in a small saucepan over high heat until it has boiled for 12 minutes. Take the pan off the heat, cool the marinade, and pour it into a sauceboat to serve at the table.

Lightly roll the turkey strips in the flour mixture. Using tongs or a slotted spatula, slip the turkey strips into the hot oil and deep-fry them until they brown on all sides, about 8 minutes.

Remove the strips and drain them on paper towels. Serve at once on a heated platter with marinade on the side.

Serves 4–6

THAT'S JUST DUCKY!

1 5- to 6-pound duck, thawed, washed, and dried

MARINADE:

1 cup shredded scallions

2 tablespoons Mirin rice wine vinegar

2 tablespoons white wine

1 tablespoon shredded fresh ginger

½ cup soy sauce

½ teaspoon ground cloves

½ teaspoon coarse salt

½ teaspoon ground cinnamon

5 teaspoons ground Sichuan peppercorn

2 tablespoons Hoisin sauce

Heat the frying oil to 375°F in a deep-frying pot.

Measure the amount of oil you'll need to cook the duck using the water method so you don't overflow oil onto the flames.

In a large bowl mix together the scallions, vinegar, wine, ginger, soy sauce, cloves, salt, cinnamon, peppercorns, and Hoisin sauce. Rub the mixture into the skin and body cavity. Cover the bowl with plastic wrap, place it in the refrigerator, and let the duck marinate overnight.

About an hour before cooking, remove the duck from the refrigerator, drain it well, pat the skin dry, and let the duck come to room temperature.

Place the duck in a steamer over high heat for 4 hours, replenishing the water as needed. Remove the duck and drain. Again, pat the skin dry.

Carefully lower the duck in a fryer basket, or on a poultry hook, into the hot oil. Deep fry it until it is brown all over, about 10 to 15 minutes. Carefully lift the fryer basket or poultry hook and remove the duck from the hot oil.

Drain thoroughly, and cut the duck into serving-size pieces, disjointing the legs and wings and cutting the breast into at least 4 sections. Serve with warm Hoisin sauce to dip.

Serves 4–6

Fish and Shellfish

BAJA-STYLE FISH BITES

MARINADE:

⅓ cup sour cream

1 tablespoon lime juice

½ teaspoon Mexene chili powder

1 pound red snapper fillets

1 cup flour

1 ¼ cups crushed corn chips

2 tablespoons melted butter

Heat frying oil to 375°F in Dutch oven or deep fryer pot.

Place 2–3 handfuls of spicy corn chips in a plastic bag, and using a rolling pin, crush them to crumb-like consistency. Pour the crumbs into a wide, flat bowl and set aside.

In a wide, flat bowl or Pyrex dish, mix the sour cream, lime juice, and chili powder with a whisk or spoon.

In another flat pan, dredge fish fillets in the flour, covering both sides of the fillets evenly.

Then soak the floured fish pieces in the marinade, again coating both sides well. Let the fish sit in the marinade for 1 to 2 minutes. Drain the excess marinade back into the bowl.

Now dredge the fish bites in the crushed corn chips, coating both sides well by pressing down on them with the back of a spoon while they are in the bowl.

Slip the fillets, no more than two at a time, into the hot oil and fry them until they are golden brown on both sides, about 3 to 4 minutes.

Serve fried fillets with a spicy tomato or fruit salsa on the side.

Serves 4

BEER-BATTERED TROUT

6 brook or rainbow trout, ¾ pound each

2 cups all-purpose flour, plus 2–3 tablespoons

2 teaspoons baking powder

1 teaspoon salt

1 tablespoon mild curry powder

2 eggs, slightly beaten

2 cups warm beer

½ cup salad oil

oil for deep-frying

fresh parsley for garnish

lemon slices for garnish

Heat the oil to 375°F in deep fryer or Dutch oven.

Wash and pat the fish dry, then put them in a paper bag with 2–3 tablespoons of flour and shake until the fish is coated with flour. Set aside.

In a large bowl combine the remaining flour, baking powder, salt, curry powder, eggs, beer, and salad oil; whisk until the mixture is smooth. Dip the floured fish into this batter, allowing the excess to drip back into the bowl.

Slip the fish into the oil and cook, turning once or twice, until golden brown on both sides, about 3–4 minutes. Remove fish from oil with a slotted spatula or frying basket. Drain on paper towels. Garnish with fresh parsley and lemon slices.

Serves 6

COCONUT-BATTERED SHRIMP

DIPPING SAUCE:

4 ounces pina colada mix

3 ounces sour cream

3 ounces drained, crushed pineapple

3 pounds shrimp, uncooked

1 ¼ cups flour

½ tablespoon baking powder

½ tablespoon salt

1 tablespoon honey granules

1 cup milk

1 whole egg

3 tablespoons melted butter

1 cup long-shredded coconut

oil for deep-frying

Heat oil to 350°F in a deep fryer or Dutch oven.

Mix the dipping sauce ingredients in a glass or stainless steel bowl and refrigerate.

Shell, clean, and devein the shrimp, but leave the tails on. Butterfly each shrimp.

Sift the flour, baking powder, and salt into a medium bowl. Add the honey granules, milk, egg, and melted butter. Whisk the mixture until smooth. Pour the coconut shreds into a wide, flat bowl or Pyrex pan.

Holding the shrimp by their tails, dip them into the batter, let the excess drip off into the bowl, then roll shrimp in the coconut to cover.

Deep fry the shrimp until golden, about 3–4 minutes. Using a frying basket or slotted spoon, remove from oil and drain on paper towels. Serve them immediately with individual bowls of the dipping sauce, which you've brought to room temperature.

Serves 6–8

DOVER CODFISH AND CHIPS

6 potatoes, approximately 1 ½ pounds

BATTER:
½ teaspoon baking powder
1 ¼ cups flour
1 teaspoon salt
½ teaspoon white pepper
1 tablespoon vegetable oil
¾ cup beer
¼ cup cream (or whole milk)
3 egg whites
1 ½ pounds cod fillets
salt to taste
lemon wedges
malt vinegar for dipping
tartar sauce for dipping

Heat the oil to 350°F in a deep-fat fryer or Dutch oven.

Peel the potatoes and square each end and sides, then cut each into ¾"
slices. Stack and cut them into ¾" sticks. Place in a bowl of ice-cold water
to soak for 30 minutes to crisp them up.

Drain the potatoes; pat VERY dry using paper towels. Dip an empty
frying basket into the oil (this prevents potatoes from sticking to it), then add
the potatoes, and lower the basket into the oil. Deep fry the potatoes till just
tender when pierced, and starting to brown, 3–4 minutes. Lift the basket
out of the oil and drain the potatoes in a basket or wire rack. They are now
partially cooked.

Sift the baking powder, flour, salt, and pepper into in a large, wide bowl.
Make a well in the middle of the flour, add the vegetable oil and beer, and stir.
Gradually add the cream (or milk) until well mixed. The batter will become

elastic. Let the batter stand for 30 to 35 minutes, till thickened.

In a copper bowl, whisk the egg whites till stiff peaks form. Gently fold the stiff whites into the rested batter, using a rubber spatula, until combined. Dip the cod fillets in the batter, turning to coat each piece thoroughly, and letting excess batter drip off into the bowl.

Using a slotted spatula, slide the fillets into the hot oil, turning once, frying 6–8 minutes until golden and crisp on the outside. Remove to a flat pan or baking sheet lined with paper towels, and keep the fillets warm in the oven (200°F) as you fry the rest.

After the fish has been cooked, place the potatoes back in the fryer basket and fry them till golden brown, about 1–2 minutes. Drain them on paper towels and place in 200°F oven to keep warm.

To serve, sprinkle the chips with salt, and decorate the fish with lemon wedges. Serve with malt vinegar and tartar sauce on the side.

Serves 6

FILLET-WRAPPED PRAWNS

Choose flat fillets of firm white fish like catfish or sole. Fillets should be thin, for they have to be rolled around the prawns.

12 large prawns
1 pound catfish fillets

BATTER DIP:

2 eggs, beaten
¼ teaspoon blackened seasoning
¼ teaspoon Louisiana Hot Sauce
½ teaspoon salt

BREADING:

1 cup flour
1 cup bread crumbs

BBQ sauce or tartar sauce for dipping
lemon wedges
oil for deep-frying

Heat frying oil to 350°F in Dutch oven or deep-frying pot.

Use a sharp knife to remove the skin from the fillets. Depending on the size of the fillets, they may then be cut into two, three, or four strips. You want strips that are at least 1″ wide.

Remove the shell the prawns and devein them. Wrap a fillet strip around each prawn and fasten it with a wooden toothpick.

Mix the beaten eggs with the blackening spices, hot sauce, and salt. Dredge the fish-shrimp rolls into the flour, coating them well with the flour. Then dip rolls into the egg mixture, and finally roll them gently into the breadcrumbs.

Using a slotted spoon, or spatula, slide the fish rolls, about 6 at a time, into the hot oil. Fry them until golden brown all over, approximately 3 minutes.

Remove them from the oil with a slotted spoon, tongs, or a spatula and drain the rolls on paper towels. Place on a cookie sheet in warm oven (200°) while the rest of the rolls are cooking.

Serve hot with BBQ sauce or tartar sauce for dipping. Arrange lemon wedges on the side.

Serves 6

HEAVENLY FRIED OYSTERS

18 large, fresh oysters, shucked
½ cup flour
2 eggs
4 tablespoons heavy cream
1 cup fine dry bread crumbs
2 tablespoons dried parsley
1 teaspoon garlic powder
1 teaspoon salt
1 teaspoon citrus pepper
oil for deep-frying
lemon wedges for garnish

In a deep-fat fryer or a Dutch oven, heat the oil to 375°F.

Put the flour in a paper bag. Drain the oysters, drop them into the paper bag, and shake them until coated with flour. Set aside on a floured plate.

Beat the eggs and cream in a shallow bowl. Combine the bread crumbs, parsley, garlic powder, and salt in another shallow bowl. Dip the floured oysters in the cream and egg mixture, then roll in the bread crumb mixture, pressing down lightly on both sides to ensure a good coating of crumbs.

For a thicker coating, repeat the process.

Fry, about 6 at a time, in the hot oil, 2–3 minutes or until golden brown. Drain them on paper towels. Serve with the lemon wedges.

Serves 4–6

OL' KING COD

1 pound cod fillets

BATTER:

1 egg

¾ cup flour

½ cup water

1 teaspoon salt

¼ teaspoon ground ginger

1 tablespoon sesame seed

½ teaspoon paprika

oil for deep-frying

Heat oil in Dutch oven to 375°F.

In a large bowl, mix the batter ingredients together, and let rest for 20 minutes to thicken.

Thaw (if frozen) or rinse (if fresh) and pat dry the cod fillets. Cut into serving-size pieces and dip the pieces into the batter. Drain them briefly but make sure each piece is coated.

Deep fry the fish in 1″ of oil in Dutch oven for 4–5 minutes each side or until golden brown.

Serves 4

PEANUT-CORNMEAL FRIED CATFISH

1 ½ pounds fresh or frozen catfish fillets

⅜ cup ground peanuts

⅔ cup yellow cornmeal

⅜ teaspoon salt

¼ teaspoon black pepper

¼ teaspoon ground red pepper

¼ cup milk

1 large egg, beaten

oil for deep-frying

Rinse the fresh fish and pat fillets dry. If frozen, thaw and rinse, then pat dry. Cut the fillets into 6 equal-size pieces.

In a wide, flat dish, combine ground peanuts, cornmeal, salt, black pepper, and red pepper. In a similar dish, combine milk and egg.

With your fingers, dip each piece of fish in the milk mixture, then roll in the nut mixture. Using your hand or a wide spoon, gently press the nuts into the flesh.

Meanwhile, in a heavy cast iron Dutch oven or deep fryer, heat 2" of oil to 375° F. Fry 1 or 2 pieces of fish at a time, about 2 minutes on each side, or until golden brown.

Carefully remove the fish with a slotted spoon and place filets on paper towels to drain. Keep them warm in a 200°F oven while frying up the remaining fish.

Serves 6

FRIED LOBSTA

4 pounds lobster tails, halved and still in shell

2 cups cornmeal

½ cup all-purpose flour

1 teaspoon paprika

1 teaspoon garlic powder

1 teaspoon onion powder

1 teaspoon lemon zest granules

½ teaspoon cayenne pepper

kosher salt to taste

lemon pepper to taste

oil for deep-frying

In a 2-gallon Ziploc plastic bag, combine cornmeal, flour, paprika, garlic powder, onion powder, cayenne, lemon zest, salt, and pepper. Shake well to mix.

Drop ½ lobster tails into the bag one at a time and shake well, until each tail is well covered with spice mixture.

Heat the vegetable oil in a deep fryer or Dutch oven to 365°F.

Slip one coated lobster tail at a time into the oil. Cook until the lobster meat turns white and the coating lightly browns. Remove lobster from oil with slotted spoon and put pieces on a paper towel covered pan in a warm oven (200°F), to drain while the rest of the tails are cooking.

Serve lobster on a heated platter with individual bowls of melted lemon-butter.

Serves 4–6

SALT & PEPPA SHRIMPS

1 pound (medium) shrimp

1 tablespoon Vodka

1 ½ teaspoons salt

⅛ teaspoon white pepper

1 cup all-purpose flour

2 teaspoons baking powder

1 cup water, cold

DIPPING SPICES:

6 tablespoons salt, kosher or coarse sea salt

½ teaspoon black peppercorns

2 tablespoons Szechwan peppercorns

2 cups oil for deep-frying

Heat the oil for deep-frying to 350°F in deep fryer or Dutch oven.

Using your fingers, carefully remove the shells from the shrimp leaving the tail intact. Devein and wash the shrimp under cold running water and then pat them dry with paper towels.

In a shallow glass or stainless steel bowl, marinate the shrimp for 10 to 15 minutes in the mixture of vodka, salt, and white pepper, turning frequently.

To make the batter put the flour and baking powder in a medium bowl and gradually add the cold water, mixing until smooth. Let the batter rest while you make the dipping spices. Combine coarse salt and black and Schezuan peppercorns in a medium bowl, then pour the salt and pepper mix into a dry skillet. Heat over high heat, stirring often, until the spices begin to brown, about 4–5 minutes.

When browned, remove the spices with a spoon and pour into a pepper grinder or counter top pulse grinder. In a pinch, you can use a clean coffee grinder just remember to run some pieces of bread through the grinder so you don't have salty or peppery coffee the next time you use it.

Take 1 tablespoon of the hot oil and mix into the batter, stirring to combine the ingredients. Take the shrimp by their tails and dip them into the batter, leaving their tails un-battered. Gently lower the shrimp into the hot oil in batches of 5–6 at a time.

Deep fry the shrimp until golden brown, about 2 minutes for each batch.

Remove from oil with a slotted spoon, drain on paper towels, and serve tails up, in a shrimp serving dish or deep soup bowl. Put the ground pepper/salt mix in small bowl and place on the table so guests can dip their shrimp into the fragrant spices.

Serves 4

SCHWIMP & KWAB WWAP

DOUGH:

2 cups white flour (unbleached preferred)

3 tablespoons oil

¾ cup water

Pinch of salt

FILLING:

8 tablespoons oil

4 cloves garlic, minced

3 medium shallots, minced

¾ pound chopped shrimp

¾ pound fresh crab meat, shredded

1 medium onion, halved and finely chopped

2 tablespoons chopped, fresh parsley

1 tablespoon curry powder

1 teaspoon paprika

4 eggs

1 stalk green onion, finely sliced

Salt and white pepper to taste

oil for deep-frying

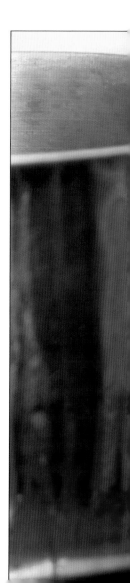

In a large bowl prepare the dough by combining all the dough ingredients and kneading them into an oily, elastic dough, about 10 minutes. Cover the dough with a moist towel and leave it at room temperature for 2–4 hours. Divide the dough into 4 pieces and roll each piece into a ball. Using lightly-oiled hands on an oiled surface, pull the dough to form 3 to 4 large (6″ diameter) circles. Evenly roll the circles flat with a rolling pin. Set aside the pieces to rest, covered and separated by layers of wax paper or aluminum foil.

While the dough is resting, heat the oil and sauté the garlic and shallots in a non-stick frying pan for a few seconds; do not let garlic turn brown.

Add the chopped shrimp and crab, and stir fry over medium high heat until the meat changes from translucent white to a solid white. Add the onion and fresh parsley and continue stir frying for another 2 minutes. Add the curry powder and paprika, stir, and cook 3 minutes. Set aside to cool to room temperature.

After mixture has cooled add the eggs, green onion, salt, and pepper to the mix, stir well, and then divide the cooked filling in four parts.

Put a thin circle of dough in the middle of a floured board, and fill one side of the dough with one of the piles of the shrimp-crab filling. Spread evenly and then brush the edges with the egg yolk-milk mixture to seal. Fold in the sides and ends to completely enclose the filling—envelope fashion.

Fry pastries in a Dutch oven or deep fryer until they are golden brown on one side, then turn and brown the other side. Remove from oil with a slotted spatula, then drain them on absorbent paper towels. Serve on a hot platter.

Serves 4

STUMPTOWN OYSTERS N' BACON

1 dozen fresh, shucked oysters, in a jar

¼ cup oyster liquor, from jar

1 bay leaf

1 teaspoon Louisiana Hot sauce

6 slices bacon

3 eggs, beaten

½ cup white flour

1 cup bread crumbs

1 teaspoon granulated garlic

12 toothpicks, for wrapping bacon

Heat frying oil to 350°F in a Dutch oven or deep-frying pot.

In a large saucepan, over medium heat, poach the oysters in the oyster liquor, with the bay leaf and hot sauce, until the edges of the oysters curl, about 1–1 ½ minutes. Remove the oysters from the liquor with a slotted spoon and set them aside. Discard the cooking liquid.

Put the eggs and flour in separate wide flat bowls. Add granulated garlic to the flour and stir well.

Cut the bacon strips in half lengthwise. Wrap each oyster with a strip of bacon and fasten it with a toothpick. Roll the bacon-wrapped oysters in the flour, dip them in the egg mixture, and then roll them in garlic-bread crumbs.

Slip the oysters into the deep fryer and cook until the bacon and oysters are browned and golden, about 4 to 5 minutes.

Remove the cooked oysters with a slotted spoon and drain them on paper towels. Serve on hot platter.

Serves 2

MANGO SALSA

¾ cup orange juice

⅛ teaspoon salt

3 tablespoons brown sugar

1 ½ cups mango, ¼" dice

3 teaspoons jalapeño (seeded and minced)

¼ bunch cilantro, chopped in large pieces

½ teaspoon black pepper

In a medium saucepan, over medium heat, reduce the orange juice, salt, and sugar until only 6 tablespoons remain. Remove from the heat and cool. When cooled, pour into a small bowl and add the mango, cilantro, jalapeño, and pepper. Mix well and chill.

Serves 6–8

WORLD'S BEST EATIN' SHARK WITH FRESH MANGO SALSA

2 pounds shark fillets (or haddock)

2 cups milk

BATTER:

1 tablespoon butter

⅔ cup Hungry Jack biscuit mix

1 teaspoon salt

½ teaspoon granulated garlic

½ teaspoon chili powder

¼ teaspoon pepper

2 tablespoons flour

Skin the fish and cut it into 3″ by 5″ pieces. Wash them under cold running water and then pat them completely dry with paper towels. In a shallow pan or baking dish, soak the fillets in milk for 2–4 hours, drain, and discard the milk. Dry and pat dry the fillets.

Heat oil to 375°F in Dutch oven or frying pot.

Melt the butter in a small pan. Mix the remaining batter ingredients in a shallow baking dish, and add the melted butter.

Put the shark fillets in a paper bag with 2 tablespoons flour, and shake until coated.

Drop 2 or 3 pieces of the fish at a time into the batter until they are well coated. Using a spoon or spatula, slip them into the hot oil.

Fry 4 to 5 minutes, or until golden brown, turning the pieces occasionally with a spoon to prevent their sticking together.

Serve with mango salsa (below).

Serves 6–8

Vegetables

BAHAMIAN PLANTAINS

4 large green plantains
1 ½ tablespoons sea salt
1 teaspoon white sugar
oil for frying

Heat oil to 375°F

Mix the sugar and salt in a small bowl and set aside.

Peel the plantains and cut them in 1″ thick slices at an angle so they are oval shaped.

Place 8–10 plantain ovals in a deep-frying basket so they are not touching, and fry them until they are slightly soft and their edges just start to brown. Remove them from the oil, drain, and cool. Fry up the rest of the plantain ovals in the same fashion.

Place the plantains on a sheet of waxed paper, cover them with another piece of waxed paper, and gently use a rolling pin or thick glass to flatten the plantains to ½″ thick.

Put plantains back into the oil and fry them approximately 3–4 minutes, until golden.

Using a large spatula or slotted spoon, remove them from the oil to some paper towels. Drain, season them with salt and sugar mix, and serve warm.

Serves 4–6

"BIG C" STUFFED PIEROGI

This is a recipe gleaned from traveling to Chicago and eating in a Polish neighborhood restaurant when I visited on several college weekends. The restaurant has faded from my memory, but the Pierogi are firmly implanted there, and in my tummy as well.

PIEROGI:

2 cups all-purpose flour

2 eggs

2 ½ teaspoons salt

⅓ cup water

CHEESE/ONION/POTATO FILLING:

½ cup chopped onion

2 tablespoons butter

½ teaspoon salt

¼ teaspoon dried chervil

¼ teaspoon dried sage

¼ teaspoon lemon pepper

2 cups mashed potatoes (instant varieties are okay)

1 cup grated sharp cheddar cheese

Heat the frying oil to 350°F in Dutch oven or deep pot fryer.

In a medium saucepan, over medium heat, sauté the onions until they are soft and translucent, but

not browned, about 5 minutes. Add the salt, chervil, sage, and pepper and stir.

Place the mashed potatoes in a large bowl and pour the onion-spice mixture over the potatoes. Add the grated cheese, and blend well with a spoon. Cover with plastic wrap and set the filling aside.

In a large pot on your stove, bring 4" to 5" of water to a boil. Add 2 teaspoons of salt.

Place the flour in a large bowl and make a "well" in the center of the flour. Break the eggs into a small bowl, and add the water and the remaining salt. Whisk the ingredients together, and then pour the liquid into the flour "well."

Using your hands, mix the flour into the liquid in the center with one hand.

Knead the dough until it's firm and well mixed. Cover the bowl of dough with a warm, moist towel, and set it aside to rest for 10–15 minutes.

Cut the dough in half. Place half on a floured board and roll the dough out to ⅛" thickness. Cover this with a moist towel and set aside. Repeat with the other half of the dough.

Using a biscuit or cookie cutter, or wide drinking glass, cut 3" circles in the dough. Repeat rolling and cutting until all the dough has been used.

Place a small spoonful of filling a little to one side of the center of each dough circle. Moisten the edge with a finger dipped in water. Fold the circles in half and pinch the edges together to seal. Then, using a fork dipped in flour, seal the edges firmly to prevent the filling from leaking out during frying.

Slide 2 to 3 Pierogi into the boiling salted water and cook for 3 to 5 minutes or until they float to the surface. Don't try to cook too many Pierogi at the same time. They will stick together and cook unevenly.

With a slotted spoon or spatula, remove the Pierogi from the water and place them in a colander to drain. Make sure they are not touching each other or they will stick together.

When well drained, place them on a piece of foil. Boil up all the remaining dumplings.

With tongs or a spatula, slide the Pierogi into the deep-frying oil, again 2 to 3 at a time, and cook until they are brown all over, about 1 to 2 minutes.

Remove them from the hot oil with a slotted spoon or spatula and serve very hot.

Serves 4–6

BUGS BUNNY FRITTERS

10 carrots, cleaned and peeled
2 eggs
3 tablespoons flour
2 tablespoons chopped peanuts
1 tablespoon brown sugar
1 tablespoon baking powder
1 tablespoon cornstarch
¼ teaspoon salt
white pepper to taste
1 cup flour
oil for deep-frying

Heat frying oil to 350°F in a Dutch oven or deep-frying pot.

In a large saucepan, over high heat, boil the carrots until tender, about 20 minutes. Place the carrots in a food processor and finely chop.

In a large bowl, add the carrots, eggs, 3 tablespoons flour, chopped peanuts, sugar, baking powder, and cornstarch. Using the pulse button, blend the mixture for about 5 seconds, then season with salt and pepper.

Form the mixture into 3" oblong fritters and dust them in the flour. Let them firm for 5 minutes on sheet of foil or waxed paper.

Carefully slip the fritters into the hot oil and cook until they begin to brown and start to float.

Remove with a slotted spoon or spatula, and drain on paper towels. Serve hot.

Serves 4–6

DOROTHY'S CORN-ON-THE-COB

6 ears of corn, shucked
12 cups water
12 tablespoons confectioner's sugar
oil for deep-frying

Heat oil in deep fryer to 300°F degrees.

Wash corn cobs and then, in a large pot, soak corn in sugar water for 1 to 2 hours. Drain and dry thoroughly.

Fry all 6 corn cobs in the oil for 3 minutes. Do not allow any of the kernels to brown during the frying. Drain the corn well in a frying basket or on absorbent paper towels.

If you use frozen corn, thaw and dry the corn thoroughly, and fry for 4 minutes.

Serve with melted butter.

Serves 4–6

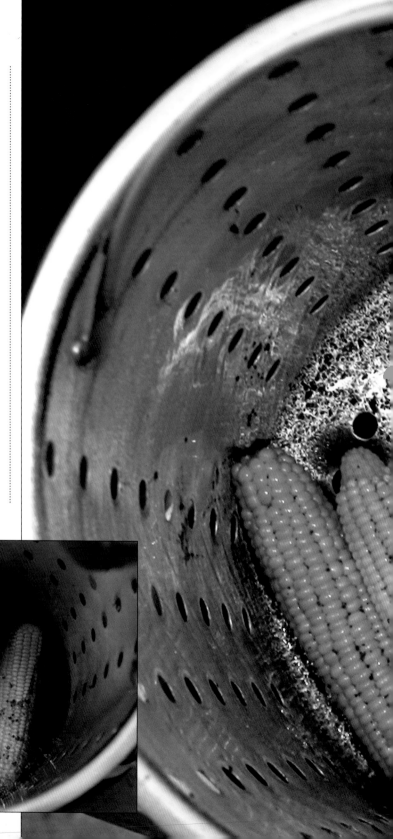

FRIED SHROOMS

BATTER:

1 cup 2 tablespoons self-raising flour

¾ cup water

2 tablespoons vegetable oil

1 pound button or crimini mushrooms

MARINADE:

¾ teaspoon onion salt

½ teaspoon Chinese 5 spices

1 tablespoon minced parsley

½ teaspoon powdered ginger

1 teaspoon rice wine

2 tablespoons self-raising flour

¾ teaspoon seasoned salt

pinch of citrus pepper

parmesan cheese to sprinkle

Heat oil in deep fryer to 375°F.

Blend the water with 1 cup of self-rising flour and stir until smooth. Let the batter stand for 5–10 minutes, and then add the vegetable oil and parsley.

While batter is resting, place marinade ingredients in a small bowl and mix well with a slotted spoon.

Remove the stalks from the mushrooms and brush off any dirt. Blanch mushrooms for 1 minute in a large saucepan of boiling water, and then drain.

Place mushrooms in a wide bowl, pour in marinade, stir, and let mushrooms rest for 15 to 20 minutes.

In a paper bag, put mushrooms and 2 tablespoons flour, and shake the bag until the mushrooms are coated. Remove them and dip them in batter using a toothpick stuck into the mushrooms. Gently slide them into the frying oil and cook until slightly brown and crispy, about 2 to 3 minutes.

Remove mushrooms from oil with a slotted spoon and drain them quickly on paper towels. Arrange the mushrooms on a plate and season them with seasoned salt and citrus pepper. Sprinkle them with Parmesan cheese and serve hot.

Serve 4–6

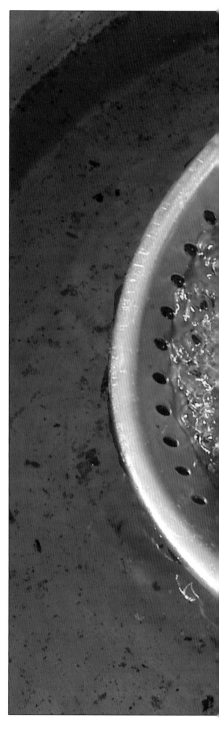

KATHLEEN'S CAULIFLOWER-ETTES

1 large cauliflower
1 quart water
1 teaspoon garlic salt
1 teaspoon paprika
1 teaspoon onion powder
oil for deep fat frying

Heat oil to 375°F in Dutch oven or deep pot fryer.

Cut away the stem, remove the green leaves, and cut the florets off the cauliflower. Discard the thick core stem.

Wash the florets under cold running water. In a large pot, bring the water to a boil over high heat, and add the salt. Drop in the cauliflower florets and cook, uncovered, for 10 minutes, or until the pieces are tender but still slightly resistant to being pierced with a fork.

Remove the florets with a slotted spoon and drain them in a colander. Pat the cauliflower completely dry with paper towels, and slip them (8 to 10 pieces at a time) into the hot oil. Fry until golden brown on all sides, about 3–5 minutes.

When they are cooked, use a slotted spoon to remove them and drain them on paper towels. Place in a warm bowl, sprinkle with the onion powder and paprika, and serve.

Serves 4–6

INDONESIAN MARTABAK

DOUGH INGREDIENTS:

2 cups white flour

3 tablespoons oil

¾ cup water

Pinch of salt

8 tablespoons oil

4 cloves garlic, peeled and sliced

2 medium-sized shallots, minced

1 medium-sized onion, halved and sliced

2 tablespoons chopped Italian parsley

1 tablespoon curry powder

4 eggs, beaten

1 stalk green onion, finely sliced

Salt and white pepper to taste

1 beaten egg

In a large bowl, prepare the dough by combining all the dough ingredients, mixing well, and then kneading the dough into an oily elastic consistency. Cover the dough with a moist towel and leave it at room temperature for 2 hours.

Divide the dough into 4 pieces and roll each piece into a ball. With oiled hands, place each piece on an oiled or marble surface and pull dough into a large, thin circle. Place finished dough circles on a plate, separated by wax paper, and set aside covered with moist towel.

While the dough is resting, make the filling. In a medium saucepan, heat the oil and sauté the garlic and shallots over medium-high heat for a few seconds. Add the sliced onion and parsley, and continue stir frying for another 2 minutes. Add the curry powder, mix well, and cook another 3 minutes. Set the filling aside to cool.

When mixture reaches room temperature, add the eggs, green onion, salt, and pepper, and mix filling ingredients well.

Heat 2 inches of oil to 375°F in a large Dutch oven. Fill the center of each of the dough circles with ¼ of the mixture. Spread the filling on one side of the dough, and brush the edges of the dough lightly with the beaten egg to help seal. Fold in the sides and ends to completely enclose the filling.

Fry the wraps in the oil until golden brown on one side, about 2–3 minutes, then turn wraps over and fry the other side. Cut the vegetable wraps into thirds and serve with curry sauce, chutney, or teriyaki sauce.

Serves 4–6

MAMA SIS'S OKRA

2 pounds okra
½ cup self-rising cornmeal
2 tablespoons self-rising flour
1 teaspoon paprika
1 teaspoon dried thyme
1 teaspoon garlic powder
¼ teaspoon cayenne pepper
dash of salt and pepper
oil for deep-frying

Heat oil in fryer to 375°F.

Wash and cut the okra into ¼" pieces. In a medium bowl, mix the cornmeal, flour, and seasonings and pour into a paper bag. Add the okra and shake the bag until all the pieces are covered with the flour mixture.

Slip the floured okra into the fryer and cook for 4–5 minutes, until the okra is browned and crisp on the outside.

Drain the okra on paper towels and serve hot.

Serves 6–8

PERSIAN DEEP-FRIED VEGETABLES

BATTER:

1 cup all-purpose flour

½ cup plain yogurt

pinch of baking powder

1 teaspoon granulated garlic

salt to taste

½ teaspoon chili powder

2 medium, thinly sliced sweet potatoes

1 medium, thinly sliced eggplant

2 medium, thinly sliced red onions

oil for deep-frying

2 fresh lemons, quartered

In a large bowl, combine the flour, yogurt, baking powder, garlic, salt, and chili powder, and let the batter rest for 10–15 minutes.

Heat the oil for deep-frying to 375°F.

Dip the vegetables in the batter to coat them evenly, drain, and gently lower them into the oil. Fry the vegetables until golden on both sides, about 2–3 minutes per side. Remove the veggies with a slotted spoon or spatula and drain them on a paper towel.

Serve hot with fresh lemon to squeeze over vegetables.

Serves 4

QUÉBEC FRENCH FRIES

For some reason the people of Québec, Canada, make "the world's best fries." They are often served in paper containers with toothpicks to pick up the fries, and with malt vinegar and salt to sprinkle over them. *Merci beaucoup*, Madame Chenvert.

12 tablespoons confectioner's sugar
12 cups water
Idaho, Bintje, or Russett potatoes
    (1–2 medium-sized potatoes per serving)
oil for deep-frying

Heat oil in deep fryer or deep Dutch oven to
    335°F.

Put 12 cups of cold water in a deep bowl, add the confectioner's sugar, and stir until the sugar dissolves, about 2–3 minutes.

Peel the potatoes, square off the ends and sides, cut into ⅜" thick slices and then cut these into ⅜" sticks.

Soak the potato sticks in a large bowl of plain water for 2–3 hours to leach out the excess starch.

Then, drain them and put them into the sugar-water, soaking them for 20–25 minutes.

Take approximately ⅓ of the potatoes and drain them (patting them dry with a paper towel is also a good idea), then place potatoes in a fryer basket. Only fill the basket about ⅓ full as the potatoes need room to cook properly. Stir with a long spoon or long tongs after 30 seconds or so.

Pre-heat oven to 200°F.

After about 2–3 minutes, the potatoes should just be getting tender and will begin to turn a light brown. Remove the fries, transfer them to a wire rack, and cool. Fry up another batch. Repeat these steps until all the potatoes are cooked, drained, and cooled.

Make sure the fryer temperature is still at 335°F.

Put potatoes back into fryer in same-sized batches as you did the first time, and fry each batch for 1 to 2 minutes. When the batches are finished, place them in the oven to keep warm until all fries are cooked.

Serve potatoes immediately, sprinkled with salt or seasoned salt. Accompany with homemade mayonnaise, a 50/50 ketchup-mayonnaise mix, or top-quality malt vinegar.

Serves 4

THE REAL FRIED GREEN TOMATOES

4 large, firm under-ripe tomatoes
1 cup polenta (or coarse cornmeal)
1 teaspoon dried oregano
½ teaspoon garlic granules
all-purpose flour for dredging
2 large eggs, beaten
salt and pepper to taste
oil for deep-fat frying

Heat oil to 375°F.

Cut the tomatoes into 1" thick slices and set aside. In a flat pan or Pyrex dish, mix the polenta or cornmeal with the oregano and garlic powder. Put the flour, egg, and polenta mix into separate bowls. Salt and pepper the slices to taste, coat them with the flour, dip the slices into the egg, and then cover both sides in the polenta.

Fry tomato slices in the hot oil in a cast iron Dutch oven or deep fryer. Cook on each side until crisp and golden brown, about 2–3 minutes. Remove slices from oil with a slotted spoon, and drain over paper towels.

Serve 4–6

WALLA WALLA ONION RINGS

4 large Walla Walla, Vidalia, or other sweet onions	1 teaspoon paprika
¾ cup all-purpose flour	1 teaspoon white pepper
¼ cup cornstarch	1 teaspoon sugar
1 teaspoon salt	1 large egg, beaten
1 teaspoon thyme	2 tablespoons vegetable oil
1 teaspoon summer savory	½ to ¾ cup dark beer
1 teaspoon onion powder	salt to taste
	oil for deep-frying

On a cutting board, cut the onions into ½" thick rings. Place the rings in cold water in a large bowl or pot and soak for 25 to 35 minutes. Drain the rings very well and pat very dry with paper towels.

In a large, flat bowl, mix in the flour, cornstarch, spices, and sugar. Then add the egg, the vegetable oil, and the dark beer, and mix gently with a large spoon until you get a thick batter. Let the batter rest at room temperature for half an hour.

In a deep fryer or Dutch oven, heat oil to 375°F. Pre-heat oven to 210°F.

Dip the onion rings into the thick batter, draining off any excess batter, then place 4 to 5 of the rings in the hot oil. Do not overcrowd, as the rings need space to cook properly and might stick together if too many are cooked at the same time. Fry the rings for 2 to 3 minutes until golden brown. Remove onions from oil with a slotted spoon or frying basket and keep them warm in the oven, on a paper towel-covered platter. Season onion rings with salt or seasoned salt and serve very hot.

Serves 4–6

WHITE CORN & SWEET PEPPER FRITTERS

1 tablespoon extra virgin olive oil

½ cup chopped sweet onion

¼ cup finely chopped red peppers

¼ cup finely chopped yellow peppers

2 cups white corn kernels, about 4 medium ears

2 tablespoons minced garlic

salt and pepper to taste

¼ cup green onions, minced

3 eggs, beaten

1 ½ cups milk

2 teaspoons baking powder

1 ¼ cups cornmeal

2 cups flour

1 tablespoon brown sugar

1 teaspoon paprika

1 teaspoon ground basil

1 teaspoon cayenne pepper

dash of hot sauce

oil for frying

Heat the oil to 375°F.

Heat the olive oil in a nonstick pan and add the onions, peppers, corn, and garlic. Season with salt and pepper, and cook for about 2 minutes.

Add in the green onions, stir, remove pan from the heat, and set it aside to cool.

In a separate bowl, beat the eggs and milk together and season with salt and pepper. Add the cornmeal, flour, brown sugar, paprika, basil, cayenne, and baking powder, whisking the mixture until the batter is smooth and free of lumps.

Pour the corn mixture into the batter, season it with a dash of hot sauce, and let the mixture rest for 10 minutes.

Using a large serving spoon, drop a heaping spoonful at a time into hot oil. When the fritters pop to the surface, use a slotted spoon to turn them over so they brown evenly on both sides. Fry 4–5 minutes, until golden brown.

Remove fritters from the oil with a slotted spoon and drain them on paper towels. Serve hot.

Serves 6–8

Desserts

DEEP-FRIED TWINKIES

2 packages of Twinkies (4 cakes)

BATTER:

2 cups flour

2 tablespoons cider or malt vinegar

2 teaspoons baking powder

1 teaspoon salt

6 ounces water

6 ounces beer

1 cup flour, for rolling Twinkies in

confectioner's sugar for sprinkling

Unwrap the Twinkies. Take a popsicle stick and shove it into one end of the cakes until there is about 2" of stick left (this will make them easier to handle during following steps). Place the Twinkies on a plate and freeze overnight.

In a large, flat bowl, mix the flour, vinegar, baking powder, salt, water, and beer together with a hand whisk until completely blended and smooth like a custard.

Remove the Twinkies from the freezer. Roll them in 1 cup of flour in a shallow pan or bowl, until they are well covered with the flour. Take the floured cakes and, using popsicle sticks to hold them, dip each cake into the batter. Coat each Twinkie well.

Slip the battered Twinkies into your deep fryer (325° to 350°F) for about 1 to 1½ minutes, or until the outside turns a nice golden brown. You'll find that the filling has just begun to melt at that point. The Twinkies tend to float, so you may wish to hold them under the oil with a slotted spoon until they brown.

Remove from the oil and let them rest on paper towels for 5 minutes (the creamy filling can be extremely hot if eaten immediately). Place the Twinkies on a warmed plate, drizzle the plate with the fruit sauce (see below), and sprinkle with the confectioner's sugar.

Serves 4

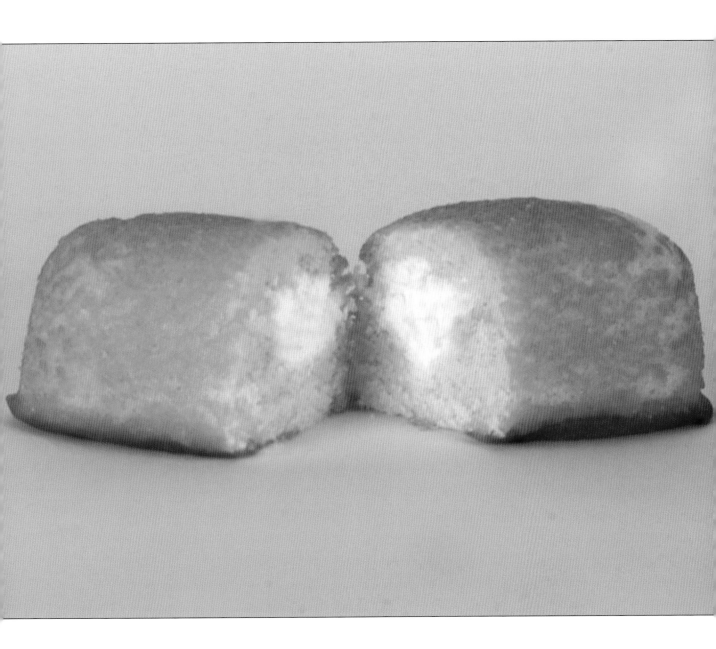

FRUIT SAUCE

1 cup chopped dried apricots

1 cup raspberries

1 tablespoon lemon juice

¼ cup fruity dessert wine (pear, apricot, or a
   favorite)

2 cups confectioner's sugar

Put the apricots, raspberries, lemon juice, wine, and sugar into a medium saucepan on medium heat and cook until it boils. Take the pan off the heat and pour the fruit mix into a small bowl, and cool until it reaches room temperature. Pour the cooled mixture into a blender or food processor and process until it is smooth, about 1–2 minutes. If you wish, you may then run the mixture through a sieve to remove the seeds. Otherwise, drizzle the sauce on the plates around the Twinkies.

Makes 1 ½ to 2 cups

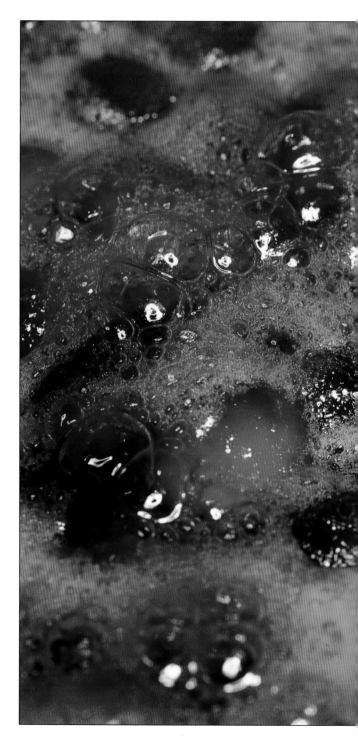

BLACK FOREST APPLE FRITTERS

1 ½ cups flour

salt

3 eggs

1 cup hard apple cider

4 Pippin, Granny Smith, or Golden Delicious
　　apples, peeled, cored, and cut into ½" slices

oil for deep-frying

½ cup confectioner's sugar

1 teaspoon cinnamon

1 teaspoon nutmeg

¼ teaspoon allspice

dash of ground cloves

Place the flour and salt in a large mixing bowl. Add the eggs and slowly stir in the cider to make a thick batter. Stir, then let the batter rest for 10 minutes.

Heat the oil to 350°F in a deep fryer or Dutch oven.

Pat the apple slices dry with a paper towel, dip the slices in the batter, and then deep fry them until golden brown (2–2 ½ minutes).

Mix the confectioner's sugar, cinnamon, nutmeg, allspice, and cloves, and put the mix in a sifter or shaker with large holes.

Serve the apple fritters warm, sprinkled with the sugar and spice mixture.

Serves 4–8

CAMEMBERT & BRIE WITH PEARS

½ pound Camembert

½ pound Brie

4 slices fresh white bread, crusts removed

2 eggs

2 tablespoons water

6 sliced pears, Bosc or Comice, OR,

6 cored and sliced apples, Pippin or Granny
    Smith, OR some of each

2 teaspoons freshly squeezed lemon juice

oil for deep-frying

Heat oil in deep fryer to 375°F.

Slice the cheeses into 12 wedges and chill them in a refrigerator for 30 minutes. Place the bread slices in a food processor and pulse until you get very fine crumbs. Place the crumbs in a shallow dish.

In a small bowl, whisk the eggs, add the water, and whisk again.

Dip the chilled cheese wedges into the egg mixture and then roll the wedges in the bread crumbs. Dip the cheese wedges again into the egg mixture, and roll in bread crumbs once more.

DO NOT USE DRIED OR COMMERCIALLY PACKAGED BREAD CRUMBS; use only fresh crumbs that you make yourself.

Place the crumbed cheese wedges on a sheet of aluminum foil and chill them for 1–2 hours. Just before cooking the cheese, slice the pears (and/or apples) and sprinkle them with lemon juice to prevent the fruit from turning brown.

Carefully place the breaded cheese wedges into hot oil for about 2 minutes or until the crumbs are golden brown. Remove with a spatula or slotted spoon and drain on paper towels. Cool slightly.

Serve warm on a platter with sliced pears.

Serves 8–10

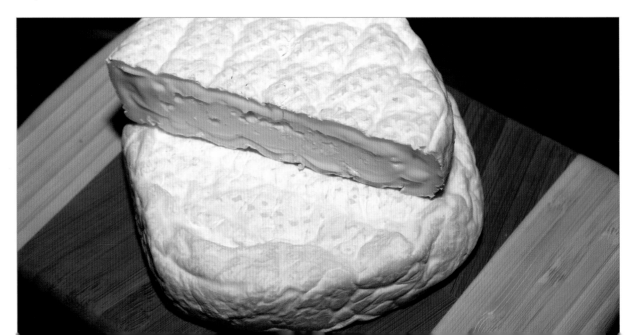

CITRUS-Y CHURROS

fresh zest of 3 lemons and 3 limes

½ cup hot water

1 stick butter, cut in 4 pieces

2 tablespoons white sugar

1 cup all-purpose flour

4 eggs, beaten

1 tablespoon granulated orange zest

1 tablespoon ground cinnamon

½ teaspoon ground nutmeg

1 tablespoon white or brown sugar

oil for deep-frying

Add lemon and lime zests to deep fryer oil while you are heating it to 375°F. When you reach that temperature, remove the fried zest with slotted spoon and discard.

In a medium saucepan, over medium heat, combine the water, butter, sugar, and flour, and stir rapidly with a wooden spoon until the mixture forms a ball that pulls away from the sides of the pan.

Take pan off the heat and beat in the eggs and orange zest. Spoon the dough into a pastry bag equipped with a large star tip (#6) and pipe a 5" to 6"-long ribbon of dough directly into the hot oil. Cut dough off with a sharp knife.

For the best results fry only a couple of Churros at a time. Cook them until golden brown, approximately 2 ½ minutes, then drain the pastry on a wire cake rack placed over paper towels.

In a small bowl or saucer, mix together the sugar, cinnamon, and nutmeg. Put mixture in a sifter and sift the spices over the hot Churros, turning to coat both sides of the pastries. Serve hot.

Serves 8–10

FRIED & CARAMELIZED APPLES

BATTER:

½ cup all-purpose flour

2 tablespoons cornstarch

¾ teaspoon baking powder

½ cup beer

2 apples, Golden Delicious or Gala

SYRUP:

⅔ cup white sugar

⅓ cup warm water

1 tablespoon salad oil

oil for deep-frying

2 tablespoons oil to use on plate

Heat oil to 350°F in Dutch oven or deep pot fryer.

In a medium bowl, mix the flour, cornstarch, and baking powder. Add the water, and with a large spoon, stir until smooth.

Peel and core the apples. Cut each apple into 4 wedges. Drop the apples into the bowl of batter and turn with a chopstick or bamboo skewer to coat evenly.

Using chopsticks or a skewer, lift one piece of fruit at a time from the bowl and let the excess batter drip off. Gently lower the apple wedge into the hot oil. Cook several pieces at a time until the coating is golden brown, about 2 minutes.

Remove the wedges with a slotted spoon and drain them on paper towels.

Fill a large serving bowl to the brim with ice cubes and cover the ice with water.

Combine the sugar, water and oil in a medium frying pan and stir to blend. Place the pan over high

heat. When the mixture begins to bubble, about 1 minute, shake the pan continuously to prevent the liquid from burning.

Continue cooking and shaking the pan until the syrup barely begins to turn a pale straw color, about 8 to 9 minutes. Immediately remove the pan from the heat. The syrup will continue to cook and it will turn golden in a few seconds.

Carefully slide the fried apples into the syrup, 2–3 at a time, and swirl the pan to coat the wedges evenly. Using two spoons, immediately remove each piece of fruit and place on a dish you've sprayed with cooking spray, making sure that the pieces do not touch.

When still hot to the touch, quickly dip each piece of fruit into the ice water so the sugar coating hardens and the fruit cools enough to eat. Serve immediately thereafter.

Serves 6

FRIED ICE CREAM–NO KIDDING!

1 pint of top-quality vanilla ice cream

3 eggs, beaten

1 teaspoon vanilla

3 cups finely crushed honey-nut cornflakes

1 cup finely crushed vanilla wafers

1 teaspoon cinnamon

vegetable oil for deep-frying

whipped cream, chocolate syrup, maraschino
    cherries (optional)

Divide the ice cream into 4 equal portions. Wearing rubber gloves, which you may keep dipping into a bowl of hot water, form the ice cream portions into 4 equal-size balls. Place them side by side, but not touching, on a freezer-safe plate, and freeze them until firm, at least one hour.

In a small bowl, beat the egg and vanilla together. In a wide, flat bowl, mix together the vanilla wafers, cornflakes, and cinnamon.

Remove the ice cream balls from the freezer. Roll each ball in the egg mixture and then roll them in the cereal mixture. Return the ice cream to the freezer.

After one hour, remove the balls from the freezer and repeat the dipping and rolling process for a second time. Make sure the ice cream is evenly covered with crumbs. If you wish, you may dip and re-roll the balls in the dry mix a third time, but usually twice is enough to obtain a good coating.

Return the ice cream balls to the freezer and leave for 3–4 hours, or ideally, overnight, until they are frozen solid.

In a deep fryer or large Dutch oven (oil must be at least 3″ deep), heat the oil to 375°F. With a large slotted spoon, slip the ice cream into the hot oil, and fry the ice cream balls 1 at a time for 15–20 seconds or until the crumbs are golden brown. Do not try to do all four ice cream balls at once, as the last one you remove may already be melting inside.

Remove the ice cream balls from the oil and drain on paper towels in a chilled dish. Serve immediately.

Garnish with whipped cream, chocolate syrup, rainbow-colored sprinkles, and maraschino cherries as desired.

Serves 4

FRIED CUSTARD SQUARES WITH LEMON-RASPBERRY SAUCE

CUSTARD:

2 cups milk

1 cinnamon stick

1 3"- to 4"-long lemon zest

6 egg yolks

⅓ cup cornstarch

½ cup sugar

½ teaspoon salt

BREADING:

2 eggs, lightly beaten

1 cup fine dry bread crumbs

1 ½ teaspoons ground cinnamon

¼ cup sugar

1 cup all-purpose flour

SAUCE:

1 ½ cups water

1 cup light brown sugar, packed firmly

½ cup light rum

fresh lemon juice to taste

fresh golden raspberries

oil for deep-frying

Butter an 8-inch-square baking pan. In a heavy saucepan, over high heat, bring the milk just to a boil with a cinnamon stick and the lemon zest floating on the surface. Keep at a bare simmer for 15 minutes. Discard the cinnamon stick and zest, then pour the hot milk through a fine sieve into a 4-cup glass measuring cup.

In a glass bowl, beat the egg yolks, cornstarch, sugar, and salt together. While slowly pouring in the milk, whisk the mixture until smooth. Pour the resulting custard into a clean saucepan, whisking continually, and bring it to a boil. Let the custard boil for 1 minute while whisking with vigor, then take it off the heat. The custard now should be smooth and thickened, and it should give off a nice cinnamon and lemon scent.

Immediately pour the custard into a prepared baking pan, smoothing the top and covering it with a piece of buttered waxed paper in which you've punched some small holes (to let any steam escape). Chill the custard in a refrigerator until firm, about 1 ½ to 2 hours. Then with a knife dipped in hot water, cut the custard into 2-inch squares.

In a small bowl mix bread crumbs, ¼ cup sugar, and ground cinnamon. In a shallow glass dish, lightly whisk 2 eggs.

Working with 1 custard square at a time, coat the custard squares with flour, shaking off the excess, and then dip them into the egg mixture, letting the excess drip off into the bowl. Gently coat the custards with the bread crumb mixture on all sides. Then transfer the coated pieces to a wax-paper-lined cookie sheet. Chill squares, uncovered for 30 minutes.

In a medium saucepan, combine the water, sugar, ½ cup rum, and simmer, uncovered, for 15 to 18 minutes. Stir in the remaining tablespoon of rum and lemon juice, and pour the mixture into a small glass bowl.

In a deep-frying pot or a heavy Dutch oven (3″ of oil), heat the oil to 375°F.

Place a cake rack in an oven set to 200°F.

Fry 2 to 3 squares until they are golden, about 15–20 seconds per side. Carefully lift the fried squares out of the oil with a spatula, whose blade had been dipped in hot oil (to prevent custards from sticking to spatula), and place the custard squares on an oven rack to drain and keep warm.

Pour a generous amount, 2 to 3 tablespoons, of sauce onto dessert plates. Place one custard square on each plate and garnish with golden raspberries.

Serves 8

MAUDIE FRICKERT'S FRIED CHEESECAKE

Cheesecake? Fried? You gotta be kidding! But no, we're not kidding! You won't believe how delicious this recipe is. Plus watching your guests' reaction when they cut into a spring roll wrapper, to discover a tasty dessert, is worth the effort.

1 medium to large cheesecake, thawed
1 cup milk (or cream)
1 egg
30 spring roll wrappers

TOPPING MIXTURE:

1 cup confectioners sugar
½ cup Nestle's Quick

Heat oil to 365°F in a Dutch oven or deep-frying pot.

Mix sugar and chocolate drink powder in flat bowl or pan, and set aside.

Cut the cheesecake into 1″ by 3″ pieces.

Lightly moisten each spring roll wrapper with beaten egg-milk (or cream) mixture.

Place a piece of cheesecake in the center of a moistened wrapper. Fold the top of each wrapper down over the cheesecake pieces, and then fold both sides toward the middle. Roll each piece of cheesecake toward you until it is completely rolled up. Gently squeeze the cheesecake rolls to make sure the dough is sealed completely.

Slip 2 to 3 rolls at a time into the oil, and allow them to brown lightly, approximately 10–15 seconds.

Using tongs or a spatula, remove the browned rolls from the oil. Place each roll in bowl of sugar-chocolate powder and turn over to coat well.

Place the deep-fried cheesecake rolls on paper towels to cool slightly before serving, about 5 minutes, as the inside will be very hot. Best served immediately after they've cooled, on a warm dessert plate. But these can also be eaten cold.

Serves 8–10

HUNGARIAN CHERRIES (OR PLUMS)

1 pound fresh ripe red cherries (or small 1"–1 ½" plums)

1 cup all-purpose flour

¼ cup sugar

⅓ cup milk

⅓ cup dry white wine

3 eggs

confectioner's sugar to sprinkle

cinnamon (or nutmeg) to sprinkle

oil for frying

Heat oil to 375°F for deep-frying.

Wash the cherries and wipe them dry. DO NOT REMOVE THEIR STEMS. Tie the stems together with thread to form clusters of three or four.

Combine the eggs, white wine, sugar, milk, and flour in a medium bowl and mix well to make a smooth batter.

Dip each cherry cluster into the thick batter, coating the cherries completely. Carefully lower cherry clusters into hot oil.

When cherries are golden, about 2–3 minutes, remove them with a slotted spoon and drain on paper towels.

Sprinkle with confectioner's sugar and a tiny bit of cinnamon (or nutmeg) on each cluster and serve warm.

Serves 6

MOMMA'S ITALIAN DESSERT PASTRIES

2 cups hot water
1 cup melted butter
2 cups all-purpose flour
1 ¼ cups granulated sugar
4 egg yolks

pinch of salt
¼ cup Marsala wine
1 teaspoon vanilla extract
1 cup cold water
oil for deep-frying
confectioner's sugar to sprinkle
honey to drizzle
granulated sugar and cinnamon to sprinkle

In a medium sized pot, heat the water and butter over high heat until boiling. Add the flour, and stir over the heat until the mixture dries and begins to pull away from the pan, about 2 to 5 minutes.

Remove the pan from the heat, and then slowly add the other ingredients, mixing them well. Form into a dough, and lightly knead for 5 minutes or so until the dough is satiny. Cover it with plastic wrap, or a moist towel, and let it sit at room temperature for 30 minutes.

Divide the dough into three parts. Take 1 part and break off small pieces from it which you can roll into a thickness about the width of your finger, by 8" long. Join the ends in a circle like a thin doughnut, moistening both ends with cold water so they'll stick together.

Fry in oil until they become golden brown, about 3 to 4 minutes. Drain on a plate covered with paper towels, and lightly dust with confectioner's sugar, sugar and cinnamon mix, or brush with melted honey.

Serves 6–8

PEACH & APRICOT FRY-PIES

PASTRY:

4 cups all-purpose flour

1 teaspoon salt

1 cup lard

1 cup milk

FILLING:

8 ounces dried apricots

1 6-ounce package dried peaches

¾ cup brown sugar

1 teaspoon vanilla

½ stick butter

1 beaten egg, with 1 tablespoon milk

confectioner's sugar

vegetable oil for frying

Heat oil in deep fryer to 325°F.

In a large bowl, mix together the flour and salt. Using forks or a pastry blender cut in the lard until the mixture is crumbly. Mix in the milk, and stir until the dough forms a ball. Cover and refrigerate the dough for 1 hour.

Remove dough from refrigerator and, using a floured cutting board, roll out the dough and cut it into 16 6" circles. Set aside.

In a large saucepan, combine the apricots, peaches, vanilla, and sugar. Add enough water to cover the fruit. Cover the pan and cook over low heat until the fruit is falling apart, about 25–30 minutes. Remove the lid and continue to cook until all of the water is evaporated. Take the pan off the heat and with a spoon stir in ½ stick butter.

Spoon equal amounts of the filling onto one half of each pastry circle and fold the circle in half. Brush egg-milk mixture on bottom edge and seal the pastry with a fork dipped in cold water.

Place in frying basket and slowly lower into the oil. Fry 1 to 2 pies at a time in the hot oil, browning them on both sides, about 2–3 minutes. Remove pies from the hot oil and drain the pies on paper towels.

While the pastry is still hot, sprinkle with confectioner's sugar.

Serves 10–12

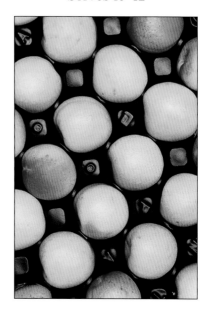

224

PETITE PEACH PIES

PASTRY:

3 cups all-purpose flour

1 teaspoon salt

¾ cup shortening, or lard

1 large egg; beaten

¼ cup water

1 teaspoon apple cider vinegar

FILLING:

4 cups chopped fresh peaches

1 cup water

1 cup peach wine

½ cup sugar

½ teaspoon ground nutmeg

pinch of ground cloves

sugar for sprinkling

In a large bowl, mix the flour and salt. Cut in the shortening with a pastry blender and blend until the mixture resembles coarse meal.

Combine the egg and water and sprinkle over the flour mixture. Add the vinegar, and stir with a fork, until the dry ingredients are moistened. Shape the mixture into a ball and wrap it in waxed paper to chill in the refrigerator for at least 1 hour.

Divide the pastry into thirds. On a floured board, roll each portion to a ¼" thickness. Cut dough into 5" circles.

Pre-heat the deep-frying oil to 375°F in a Dutch oven or deep-frying pot.

Combine the peaches, water, and wine in a large saucepan and bring to a boil over high heat. Reduce the heat, cover the saucepan, and simmer until tender, about 20 minutes.

Cool the peaches and mash them slightly with a potato masher or large spoon. Stir in the sugar, nutmeg, and cloves, and set aside.

Place about 2 tablespoons of the peach mixture on half of each pastry circle. To seal the pies, dip your fingers in cold water and moisten the edges of the pastry circles. Fold the circles in half, making sure the edges are even. Press the edges of the filled pastries firmly together using a fork dipped in flour.

When all the pies are made, slip 1 or 2 at a time into the hot oil. Fry the pies until they are golden brown on both sides, about 4 to 5 minutes, turning once.

Drain the pies well on paper towels. Sprinkle them with sugar while the pies are still very warm, and serve.

Serves 6–12

RB'S KEY LIME CRULLERS

1 cup water

¼ cup lard

2 tablespoons granulated sugar

½ teaspoon salt

1 ¼ cups all-purpose flour

4 eggs

1 tablespoon grated lime zest

oil for deep-frying

LIME GLAZE:

3 cups powdered sugar

1 teaspoon grated lime zest

4 tablespoons lime juice

powdered sugar in sifter

lime granules

Heat oil in deep fryer to 375°F.

With scissors, cut out 12 4″ by 4″ squares of aluminum foil, and generously brush one side of each square with vegetable oil. Using a 2 ½″ round cookie cutter, score the center of each foil sheet for a guide to shape the crullers. Put foil on baking sheets.

In a large saucepan, combine the water, lard, sugar, and salt and bring to a full rolling boil over high heat. Quickly add the flour and beat vigorously with a wooden spoon until the dough forms a ball and pulls away from the pan. Remove the pan from heat.

Make a well in the center of the dough and add the eggs, beating with a wooden spoon after each egg is added, until the pastry is mixed, and is smooth and satin-like. Add the lime zest and mix well into the dough with a spoon.

Put the warm dough in a large pastry bag. With a ½″ large star-tip in place, squeeze the dough into circles onto the oiled and scored foil, using the circular marks on the foil to make round circles of dough. Let the dough circles cool in the refrigerator for 15–20 minutes.

Slide the dough circles off the foil into hot oil. Fry the crullers for 4 to 5 minutes, turning them several times, until both sides are brown and crullers puff up. Remove crullers with a wire net or slotted spatula, and drain them on paper towels.

Mix the glaze ingredients together in a shallow, wide bowl. Dip the crullers halfway into glaze, and then let excess glaze drip back into the bowl. Place crullers glazed side up on a wire rack until the glaze sets. Sprinkle with powdered sugar and some of the powdered lime granules.

Serve crullers warm, with strong coffee.

Serves 6–8

SONGKRAN BANANA FRITTERS

6 small, half-ripe bananas
lemon juice

BATTER:

½ cup all-purpose flour
2 tablespoons cornstarch
¼ cup granulated sugar
½ cup water
¼ teaspoon salt
1 teaspoon banana liqueur
½ cup shredded coconut
Canola oil for deep-frying
powdered sugar & cardamom in shaker

Peel the bananas and cut them crosswise into 3" to 4" lengths. Brush them with lemon juice so they won't turn brown, and set aside.

In a medium bowl, sift together the flour, cornstarch, sugar, and salt. Add the water slowly while stirring constantly with a large spoon, add liqueur, then continue to stir until the batter is smooth and thick enough to lightly coat the back of a spoon. Add the coconut and gently fold it into the batter.

Heat oil in a deep fryer or Dutch oven (3" of oil) to 375°F.

Slide the bananas into the batter. Using a long bamboo or metal skewer, lift out the coated banana pieces one at a time, allowing the excess batter to drop into the bowl. Carefully lower each piece of banana into the hot oil. Do not fry more than 3 to 4 pieces at a time as the fruit must be able to float freely.

Deep fry, turning often with chopsticks or a slotted spoon, until golden brown, about 2 to 2 ½ minutes. Drain fried bananas on paper towels, and place on a platter in a 200°F oven to keep warm.

Repeat with the remaining pieces of banana.

Arrange the bananas on a lettuce leaf, on a warmed platter, and sprinkle them with confectioner's sugar to which you've added a pinch or two of cardamom.

Serves 6

Batter UP!

**HERE ARE FOUR BATTERS TO USE WHEN
DEEP-FRYING FISH, FRUIT, POULTRY, OR MEAT.**

BRINY BEER BATTER

1 cup cornstarch

1 cup all-purpose flour

1 tablespoon garlic powder

1 tablespoon green onion powder

1 tablespoon lemon granules (or zest)

1 tablespoon lemon (or citrus) pepper

1 tablespoon coarse salt

1 bottle of your favorite beer

1 cup of all-purpose flour for dredging

In a large bowl, mix all the ingredients together and whisk together until fully integrated. Chill for 20 minutes in a refrigerator.

Pour the second cup of flour into a wide shallow bowl and dredge fish in the flour. Then dip the fish fillets or steaks into the batter mix and let the excess drip back into the bowl. Fry and enjoy.

SWEET MARY'S FRUIT BATTER

2 large eggs
1 tablespoon vegetable oil
½ cup buttermilk
2 tablespoons heavy cream
1 cup flour
¼ cup sugar
1 teaspoon baking powder
1 teaspoon salt
1 teaspoon vanilla extract
1 cup all-purpose flour for dredging.

In a large bowl, mix all the ingredients together and whisk until fully mixed and batter is smooth. Set aside in a refrigerator for 20 minutes to set. Pour the second cup of flour into a shallow dish and use to dredge fruit pieces. Dip the floured fresh fruit into the batter, let excess drain off, and fry.

BIRD FRYIN' BEER BATTER

1 ½ cups all-purpose flour

1 teaspoon cornstarch

1 tablespoon paprika

1 teaspoon onion powder

1 teaspoon salt

½ teaspoon pepper

1 bottle or 12-ounce can of your favorite beer

1 cup all-purpose flour for dredging

Sift the flour, paprika, onion powder, salt, and pepper into a wide, flat bowl. Add the beer, stirring with a wire whisk until well mixed, frothy, and smooth. Let the mixture cool in a refrigerator for 30 minutes just before using whisk once more to make sure mixture is well incorporated.

Dredge chicken pieces with flour and then into batter, draining off excess. Deep fry and enjoy.

NACOGDOCHES STEAK DIP

1 cup all-purpose flour

½ cup cornstarch

1 teaspoon oregano

1 teaspoon chili powder

1 teaspoon baking powder

1 teaspoon powdered garlic

1 cup cold water

1 tablespoon vegetable (or olive) oil

1 cup all-purpose flour for dredging

Place all of the dry ingredients into a wide, flat bowl and mix well. Add the water and oil and stir until thoroughly mixed.

Dredge steaks or fillets in the flour then dip them into the batter; it should be quite thick. Fry and enjoy.

Conversion Charts

METRIC CONVERSION CHART

US	Canadian
¼ teaspoon	1 mL
½ teaspoon	2 mL
1 teaspoon	5 mL
1 tablespoon	15 mL
¼ cup	50 mL
⅓ cup	75 mL
½ cup	125 mL
⅔ cup	150 mL
¾ cup	175 mL
1 cup	250 mL
1 quart	1 liter

Temperatures	
Fahrenheit	Celsius
32°	0°
212°	100°
250°	120°
275°	140°
300°	150°
325°	160°
350°	180°
375°	190°
400°	200°
425°	220°
450°	230°
475°	240°
500°	260°

Weight	
Ounces	Grams
1	30
2	55
3	85
4	115
8	225
16	455

"THE REAL" METRIC CONVERSION CHART

10^{12} microphones = 1 megaphone

10^6 bicycles = 2 megacycles

2000 mockingbirds = 2 kilomockingbirds

10 cards = 1 decacards

½ lavatory = 1 demijohn

10^6 fish = 1 microfiche

454 graham crackers = 1 pound cake

10^{12} pins = 1 terrapin

10 bowling pins = a strike

10^{21} picolos = 10^9 los = 1 gigolo

10 rations = 1 decoration

100 rations = 1 C-ration

10 millipedes = 1 centipede

3 ⅓ tridents = 1 decadent, or one large mouthful of gum

5 dialogues = 1 decalogue

4 travels = 1 travelogue

4 grammys = 1 grammaphone, or 4 gold records

8 nickels = 2 paradigms

2 snake eyes = 1 paradise

1 drake and one hen = 1 paradox

10^2 mental = 1 centimental

10 ornis = 5 ornamentals

10^1 mate = 1 decimate

10^{12} bulls = 1 terabull

10^{12} boos = 1 picoboo

Located on the Diamond Bar (CA) High School Web site http://dbhs.wvusd.k12.ca.us/Humor/ - designed by chemistry teacher John Park and the Chem Team.

THE FREQUENT FRYER FLYIN' FICKLE FINGER OF FÊTE AWARDS

Linda Myers, MyComm
Dr. John Davis
Milan Chuckovich
Pat & Tara Bennet
Patty Boday, Oregon Spice
Jeff Tracy
Brian Coleman, Char-Broil
Grigory Zaychick
Michael Armstrong, Swine & Dine
Patrick S. Terveer, Georgie Boy
Linda Lutes
Loretta Barrett Oden, Corn Dance Cafe
Charles Charbonneau
Jim Kurfurst, Butcher Boys
Ken Haviland, Real Canadian Bacon Co.
Aliza Fogelson
Angelica Canales
Judith Regan
Mike Starks, Soha Sign
Misty River
Carolyn Wells

Ardie Johnson
Paul Kirk
Smokey Hale
John Willingham
David Klose
The Car Dogs: Jack Rogers & Jim Minion
Amy Anderson & Mad Momma
Jon & Jana Trueb
Rocky Danner, National Barbecue News
Garry Howard, The Smoke Ring
Randall Oliver, Smart & Final
Chris Sandberg, Have Smoke Will Travel
Chef Jamie Gwen
Cody Oliveira
Barry Pelts, Corky's
Michael R. Parr
Rubie Lloyd, Chefwear
Michelle Rosa, Chefwear
Carl Raymond
Kathy Browne
Chris Browne
Kara Browne
Tricia Kawahara
Tom Ryll
Barbara Johnson
Nathan Wu
Steve Lane

Index